Crawling Behind

America's Childcare Crisis
and How to Fix It

Elliot Haspel

Black Rose Writing | Texas

ISBN: 978-1-68433-427-8
PUBLISHED BY BLACK ROSE WRITING
www.blackrosewriting.com

Printed in the United States of America
Suggested Retail Price (SRP) $16.95

Crawling Behind is printed in Plantagenet Cherokee

To Melissa, my sun; Alma and Esther, our ever-spinning planets.

Introduction - "The Conversation"

As my wife and I prepared for the arrival of our first daughter, we sat down and had The Conversation. Not about baby names or managing in-laws, but the conversation happening over steaming boxes of takeout throughout wide swaths of America: How in the world are we going to pay for childcare?

Childcare is perhaps the most vexing budgetary challenge facing today's young American families. It's causing enormous strain on both parents and kids. It also carries a triple threat to American society writ large. The lack of affordable, accessible, high-quality care is simultaneously an anchor weighing down the mobility of both the middle and lower income classes; an economic dagger that keeps more than a million people – especially women – out of the workforce; and a plague on the nation's future as untold millions of children miss out on optimal development during the brain's most critical growth period.

By the way, while the early childhood field prefers the more precise terms "early care and education" or "early childhood education," I've opted for the more commonly used lay term "childcare."* I use "childcare" (sometimes shorthanded to "care") to refer to all caregiving settings, primarily focusing on non-parental care during the first five years of life. This includes what is variously known as preschool or pre-Kindergarten. We'll also talk plenty about stay-at-home parents, and talk briefly about care for school-aged kids. As we'll see, "care" and "education" in early childhood are largely synonymous.

Truth be told, childcare costs may eventually pose a fourth, more existential threat to the United States: Birth rates have steadily declined to a 30-year low. In a 2018 survey commissioned by the *New York Times*,

---

* The field also prefers to render the term as two words, "child care," a la health care or elder care. I've chosen to use the one-word version for readability. One last terminology note: throughout the book I'll use the word "parents" as shorthand for "parent(s)/guardian(s)." It's intended to be inclusive of children being raised by grandparents, foster parents, etc.

the top reason childbearing-age adults gave for having fewer children than they would otherwise want – a reason cited by fully two-thirds of respondents – was the cost of care.[1]

The governmental and societal responses to this crisis have been anemic. Weak subsidies for families in poverty don't cover the full cost of care and have absurd, years-long waiting lists.[2] The federal child-related tax credits cap out at a mere fraction of what parents pay. We're fighting a five-alarm fire with the public policy equivalent of beach toy water buckets.

There is a solution. It's relatively simple: start treating childcare like America's universal public education system – a common good, easily accessible and free for families.

In an instant, we'd be removing a crippling financial boulder from the backs of tens of millions of Americans while supercharging the economy and the brain architecture of the nation's next generation. It would simultaneously be one of the greatest pro-family and anti-poverty tools ever wielded. We'd also be injecting enough funding into the system to allow for a functional and high-quality childcare marketplace, including paying critically important teachers a decent wage instead of paying them on par with parking lot attendants.[3]

Unlike the public K-12 system, the needed flexibility of care during the first five years demands a more portable approach. Thus, we should give every family an annual Child Development Credit of $15,000 or so per child*, and let them use it on care during the birth-to-five years. We should further provide a Youth Development Credit of $1,000 or so during the five-to-eighteen years to help cover before/after-school and summer care.

We've shifted our society's idea of what deserves public support many times before. We can do it again, and we can do it now.

*   *   *

Big societal changes tend to occur in a state of 'punctuated equilibrium,' to borrow a term from evolutionary biology: long periods of little-to-no change followed by spikes of massive change. A good example of this is American enrollment in high schools. From 1910 to 1940, the percentage of American teenagers enrolled in high school leapt from 18

---

* Cost-of-living adjusted, and indexed to inflation

percent to 71 percent.[4] In the entire 19th century, the enrollment percentage had barely budged. This was a tectonic shift in the very structure, rhythm, and expectations of American life, and it happened in a generation.

Similarly, the GI Bill (technically the "Servicemembers Readjustment Act") reshaped American higher education as the country emerged from World War II. That conflagration ended in 1945. By 1947, nearly half of college admissions belonged to veterans.[5] Almost eight million WWII veterans went to college utilizing the GI Bill, in the process spurring the mass normalization of college and the strengthening of public colleges and universities.

Why do these spikes happen? At the simplest level, the pressure becomes too intense to accommodate incrementalism. The rapid industrialization of America in the late 19th and early 20th centuries led to a clamor from businesses for more educated individuals. The GI Bill, meanwhile, was largely designed out of a cold-sweat terror of what to do with 16 million returning soldiers and wanting to avoid the crises that followed from not having a plan for World War I veterans.[6] In other words, due to a combination of external forces, pressure starts building rapidly, and society can either find a way to vent it or can deal with the consequences of the explosion.

The impacts of these spikes are not just felt on the particular people they're designed to help, such as teenagers or veterans; the impacts are communal. A bumper crop of high school students meant buildings and roads needed to be constructed, teachers and other staff needed to be hired. A flood of new college students meant that there needed to be dorms and instructors to accommodate them – enrollment at the University of Miami (FL) more than tripled in two years! – and in many cases new institutions of higher education altogether. In 1944 there were 58 community colleges in America — three years later, 328.[7]

It's important to remember is that these shifts were *expensive,* and government at different levels – via taxpayers – was footing the bill. In the first five years of the GI Bill alone, the federal government shelled out (in today's dollars) over $14 *billion* in college tuition and living stipends. Localities across the country raised taxes to fund their new high schools since during that era there was weak state and federal K-12 support.

Why were taxpayers willing to pay into this system, even if they didn't have children or veteran kin? Going all the way back to Thomas

Jefferson's 1779 *Bill for the General Diffusion of Knowledge*, there have always been three philosophical tracks to why society supports free public education (at least for some populations; there is, of course, a twisted vine of racial and gender discrimination embedded in this history). In the High School Movement, in the GI Bill, in the more recent expansions of Kindergarten and pre-Kindergarten, these tracks align with varying intensities.

The first is a democratic ideal, the poetic notion that an educated citizen is a constructive citizen, and that civic discourse requires citizens who have the wherewithal to engage.

The second is an economic ideal, the capitalist notion that our economy only thrives when there are workers who are educated enough to fill the jobs and produce lucrative innovations.

The third is a utilitarian ideal, the functional notion that while education is all well and good, school is, crucially, a place for children to be so that their parents can go to work.

The pressure is building again, this time around the inordinate cost of childcare and a hopelessly broken childcare marketplace. Again, the three philosophical tracks are aligning. Again, we face a crossroads: Alter our societal commitments in the face of new needs, or contend with the volcano's wreckage.

*   *   *

Everyone knows childcare is expensive. The ragged state of current affairs may still cause bile to rise.

Around two-thirds of American children under the age of six have all available parents/guardians in the workforce, meaning they need some amount of non-parental care.[8] Yet childcare is more expensive than in-state college tuition in 28 states and Washington, D.C.[9] Nationally, the average for one child across all types of paid care – centers, home-based, churches, nannies, etc. – falls somewhere around $9,500 a year, with many states' averages significantly higher. For infants, because the adult-to-child ratio must be so much lower, the annual costs quickly jump to *$15,000* or more*. With two kids in care, the

---

* Massachusetts leads the pack at an almost impressive $20,415 average for one infant in full-time center care.

costs can easily exceed, if not double, monthly rent or mortgage payments!

Yet costs are continuing to rise, and childcare spending is *far* outpacing wage growth. The divergent lines illustrate a grim trajectory. Since 1985, families' average childcare spending has nearly doubled – and the rate of spending growth is only speeding up – while workers' median weekly earnings have barely budged.[10]

This is not just a 'poor people's problem'. This is a problem for the three-quarters of Americans who make less than $100,000 a year (and, absurdly, it's a problem for a decent number of those who make six-figures, particularly in more expensive cities like New York City or San Francisco). It also reflects what analyst Matt Bruenig calls a "lifecycle income problem," which is the simple fact that we make the highest salaries from when we're middle-aged on, but have children when we're young(ish).[11]

What's more, these cost averages do not consider quality, nor do they lead to fiscal sustainability on the part of the childcare providers. As detailed later, we're tapping out parents while providers can barely make enough money to keep their doors open and are forced to pay their employees next to nothing.

Social mobility – the ability to rise effortfully through income brackets – is the hallmark of the American Dream. Social mobility requires the generation of wealth, and wealth is built through investments such as owning a house, stocks, etc. Wealth generation also requires having a manageable amount of debt. Childcare costs are vacuums sucking up middle- and lower-class income that would otherwise go to this wealth creation and debt repayment.

It can be unsettling to realize the extent to which childcare costs are forcing the deferral of goals, even among college-educated, married, dual-earner couples. Alyson Williams lives in Richmond, Virginia with her husband, where she works for a nonprofit organization, and he works as a data analyst. Her two-year-old son attends a local center between 25 and 40 hours a week. This should be a reasonable setup: a two-income household in a moderate cost-of-living city, and only one child. Yet, Alyson explains that, "as a middle-income family with other costs like a mortgage, student loans, aging parents, etc., childcare eats up – or exceeds – our income pretty quickly. There are times when we have other large expenses like taxes, required travel, home repairs, etc., when we end up putting all or most of our childcare costs on a credit card with an ever-increasing balance." Perhaps most poignantly, Alyson notes that were it not for their son's childcare costs, "it's very likely we would have more than one child."

Welcome to the volcano.

Consider a family with two children, spaced say three years apart. That's eight years spent paying out the nose for care (ignoring for a moment the not-insignificant costs of after-school and summer care for school-aged kids). Nearly a decade of escalating debt, deferring needed house and car maintenance, missed opportunities for savings and investments and pursuing business and career opportunities — to say nothing of pursuing personal passions or the other elements that lead to thriving rather than surviving.

And, that, of course, is the *best-case scenario* where the family can actually 'afford' to shell out for care.

* * *

For many families with lower incomes – and America's legion of single parents – these childcare costs can be literally prohibitive. The money doesn't exist, and there may be no grandparents nearby to tap, especially given lower life expectancies and higher rates of disabling illnesses among the poor. So, what are the options?

Option one: a parent doesn't work or takes on a highly undesirable work situation, such as a lower-paying, part-time, and/or graveyard shift job, burdening the family yet more[*].

Option two: the family is forced into patching together a highly undesirable childcare situation, perhaps paying a modestly-known neighbor under the table to stick the kids in front of a screen for hours on end.

This is a massive problem. An analysis by the Center for American Progress revealed that "in 2016 alone, nearly 2 million parents of children age five and younger had to quit a job, not take a job, or greatly change their job because of problems with childcare."[12] Among poor nonworking parents with young children, more than 70 percent are staying home primarily to take care of the family[†].[13] Indeed, if childcare was not a barrier, one-in-three unemployed parents would seek to rejoin

---

[*] On the flip side, a parent who wants to stay home and raise their children may be forced to take a job, despite the fact that the vast majority of earnings will go towards childcare costs.

[†] The bulk of the rest are disabled or in school.

the workforce.[14] Put simply, childcare costs are a significant and *direct* cause of poverty.[15]

Even for those parents who do work outside the home, shaky childcare situations cause huge amounts of lost productivity. Nationally, businesses lose out on nearly $13 billion every year because of employees missing work due to childcare breakdowns, while workers themselves – because this disproportionately impacts hourly workers with little-to-no leave time – drop more than $8 billion of lost wages on the floor*.[16] One study found that "an overwhelming 86 percent of primary caregivers said problems with childcare hurt their efforts or time commitment at work."[17]

Businesses have started to notice: In early 2019, the Council for a Strong America's ReadyNation initiative, a bipartisan coalition of over 2,000 executives, released a report with the blunt title, "Want to Grow the Economy? Fix the Childcare Crisis."[18]

And, in the absolute worst-case scenario, these impossible choices laid at the feet of stretched, stressed-out parents lead to the unthinkable: children in unlicensed, unregulated care situations suffering abuse and even death.[19]

* * *

While all of this would be bad enough on its own, it's happening during the most critical period of brain development in a child's life.

The first five years of life hold a breathtaking amount of brain growth: the youngest among us are making more than one million neural connections every *second*.[20] These are the literal building blocks of intelligence, compassion, and creativity, all of the foundational features of future workers, citizens, and inventors. What overwhelmingly determines whether a child develops optimally or sub-optimally is the quality of her interactions with her caregivers. In 2000, an expert panel of researchers put it this way in a 600-page research report called, fittingly, *Neurons to Neighborhoods*:

"The scientific evidence on the significant developmental impacts of early experiences, caregiving relationships, and environmental threats

---

* Workers also give up another $5.5 billion due to unpaid or partially paid parental leave immediately following the birth of a child, a topic that will be touched on in a later chapter.

is incontrovertible. Virtually every aspect of early human development, from the brain's evolving circuitry to the child's capacity for empathy, is affected by the environments and experiences that are encountered in a cumulative fashion, beginning early in the prenatal period and extending throughout the early childhood years."[21]

Anyone who has spent time around young children intuitively understands the importance of relational interactions. The crying child who lets himself be distracted when his parent leaves the room because on some level his brain is confident Mom or Dad will return soon enough; the toddler who exclaims at seeing a squirrel out the window and instantly swings her head to look expectantly at you, ready to have a conversation about this thrilling development in her day.

Yet for all that importance, the childcare business is a raw deal all around. Childcare providers, with the exception of federally-funded Head Start or pre-K that is part of the public school system (keep these important exceptions in mind as we move through the book), struggle mightily. Driven largely by the need for low adult-to-child ratios – in most states, a teacher of infants can legally care for four or five children, while a 4th-grade teacher can care for 25 or more* – providing childcare has extremely high fixed costs. Yet providers are beholden to what early childhood finance experts term "The Iron Triangle" – they will fail to stay in the black unless they are constantly at full enrollment, they set their tuition rate high enough to cover costs, and they collect tuition on-time from all families. This is an immensely difficult feat of geometry.[22]

As a result of these wafer-thin margins, providers have to cut their human capital costs to the bone. Nationally, center teachers make an average of $10.72 an hour – about $22,000 a year – putting them in the whopping 2nd percentile of wage earners†.[23] In contrast, elementary school teachers make an average of $32.98 an hour (and should make more). Remember how important early childhood practitioners are for the development of the children who are with them hours on end. Yet over half(!) of all childcare workers make such low wages that they are forced to utilize some form of public assistance (SNAP, Medicaid, etc.).

As the National Association for the Education of Young Children

---

* I'm not suggesting high class sizes in K-12 are good, simply that it's an important contextual difference between the age groups. When I taught 4th grade, I maxed out at 33 children stuffed into my classroom; way too many!
† Another fun fact: As of 2013, median wages for full-time childcare workers hadn't increased in the last twenty years.

puts it, we've reached a situation where "parents can't pay more, educators can't make less."[24]

The problem can be summed up in one sentence: There is not enough money in the system.

The center – or, perhaps more aptly, the centers – cannot hold.

*   *   *

This book is laid out in three broad sections.

The first section looks at the building blocks of the current crisis. It traces the divergent histories of the American public education system and childcare (non-)system to see how we've arrived at this moment. We'll look at the different ways each system is paid for, and why every argument for funding free K-12 common schools also applies to providing Credits during the first five years. We'll consider the rainbow of different ways we deliver childcare in America, and how the marketplace of those options is in a state of what economists would consider complete market failure. Finally, we'll delve into the practical and consider how a robust childcare Credit system would work, including the important question of what this means for stay-at-home parents (spoiler alert: it means they finally get compensated for their work). Common means common, by the way; just as Bill Gates can send his kids to public school for free or walk through Central Park for free, the Credits need to apply across the board.

The second section goes deep into how Child Development Credits would transform the childcare system. We'll explore what childcare quality means in different settings, and paint the picture of healthy options across formal-, informal-, and parent-provider care. We'll also look at what fixing the childcare crisis will mean not just for the young children, but for their families and care providers alike.

The third section is devoted to answering the key and oh-so-simple question: How are we going to accomplish this? We'll tackle head-on the question of paying for zero-cost childcare, and we won't shy away from getting political. We'll show that affordable, high-quality childcare is one of the few remaining bipartisan issues, and we'll chart a path to making universal childcare a reality. In the past fifty years, there has been no more promising time for making a structural change in childcare: just during the writing of this book, major childcare pushes have emerged from sources as disparate as U.S. Sen. Elizabeth Warren (D-MA) and

Ivanka Trump[*]. We'll also pull back and talk about a package of additional family supports that, while more modest, are necessary to enable less affluent families to thrive and take full advantage of high-quality childcare. Foremost among these is an unrestricted child allowance (essentially, funds for families to meet their kids' basic needs). Lastly, we will consider the implications of family-friendly policies for the very future of families, communities, the nation, and, without hyperbole, the world.

The time for incremental solutions has passed. We are not approaching a crisis point, we are in the middle of the crisis right now, here today. Children are a joy, and fitting them into our lives and our society should not be a terror. There is only one true solution, as simple and transformative as the High School Movement or the GI Bill. The solution, in fact, traces its roots all the way back to the 19th-century advent of mass common schools:

Childcare should be free for families.

A Note on Proposals

Writing a book with specific policy proposals, to the point of putting numbers down, is a dangerous proposition.

Ask people if they generally support an idea, let's say their local government spending more on parks, and most will agree. Start asking if they support raising X tax or imposing Y fee to pay for it, or start talking about what part of town it will be in (not theirs), and support plummets. Similarly, I'm sure even as you were reading the introduction, objections started to form in your mind – where did he come up with $15,000? How are quality controls going to work? Won't this incentivize people to stop working? (OK, well, I can answer that one now: No. Except for maybe moms who just delivered a watermelon-sized human and would like some time to recover and bond). What about messy situations where divorced parents split custody of their kid? And so on.

These critical questions are good. Public policy is formed by what Otto Von Bismarck famously called "the art of the possible – the art of the attainable, the next best."[25] In other words, politics is compromise. I

---

[*] Similarly, throughout the book I utilize sources from both sides of the aisle, such as the conservative American Enterprise Institute and the liberal Center for American Progress.

have no doubt that the first city or state to adopt some form of universal free childcare will have a program that looks rather different in specifics than what I'm proposing here. That's good; that's the way it should be.

I am choosing to lay out a specific proposal rather than an abstract concept because this is a serious, sober suggestion, not an idealist's fever dream. If I can get you to arguing the specific amount of the Credit and how it would be implemented, then that means I've made my case because *you agree that universal free childcare is needed.* The devil may be hiding in the details, but the current state of childcare is a hellmouth we must pass through first (lest you think I'm overdramatic, a 2013 *New Republic* investigative cover story was literally called "The Hell of American Day Care").[26]

To illustrate that this isn't about any given proposal, I've also included a brief chapter preceding the conclusion called "Variations on a Theme," which offers the broad strokes of a few alternatives. Most notable, perhaps, are two variations. First, providing different Credit amounts for each age band; second, a mixed system where care is delivered to infants and toddlers via Credits while three- and four-year-olds are offered a system of universal public childcare centers (i.e. "universal pre-Kindergarten").

All this preamble is to ask one thing of you as a reader, a compact of sorts before we dive in. Try to not get so caught in the specifics of what I'm proposing that you miss the underlying question – should childcare be free for families?

A Note on Stories

All the stories featured in this book are true, including the ones about my own family. Information was gathered via interviews in the Fall of 2018 and reflect the realities for individuals and couples at that time. In several cases, people's names have been changed at their request to ensure their comfort in sharing what can often be uncomfortable truths about their financial and childcare situations. I have noted when pseudonyms are in use. No information other than names has been altered.

SECTION I: SETTING THE STAGE FOR CHANGE

The American childcare crisis is complex, with many moving and interlocking elements ranging from historical to economic to sociological. We're going to cover a lot of ground in this first section, so as a sort of 'compass,' I've developed the following diagram to summarize what we'll discuss. If your head starts to spin, feel free to refer back to it as a touchstone:

Compass Rose of the American Childcare Crisis

More families needing outside care as economic pressures and changing family preferences drive ongoing increases in dual-worker households

Rising costs of care due to higher rents + health & safety regulations; lessened ability of Millenial parents to pay due to stagnant wages, student loans, health care, etc.

Most Critical Years For Foundational Brain Development

Providers unable to stay solvent = low staff wages, reduced quality, increased closures, & the rise of child care deserts

Extremely limited public investment due to historical disdain for mothers working & misunderstandings of early childhood development

Chapter 1: Why *Isn't* Childcare Free for Families?

The Breadth of the Crisis

Carey and Yuan Tang are doing everything right. Carey worked her way through one of the top-ranked high schools in America and the University of Virginia before landing back in the Washington, D.C. area. Along the way, she got an MFA and MBA in New York City, where she met and married Yuan, who has made a career for himself as a first-rate chef with a pedigree from famous Michelin-starred NYC establishments like Jean Georges. The pair of 31-year-olds recently launched their own restaurant, Rooster & Owl, while Carey also maintains a nine-to-five job doing fundraising work at a local children's hospital (hence the name – Carey's up with the morning sun while Yuan works nights).

Well educated. Hard-working, talented professionals from different backgrounds. Entrepreneurs. The Tangs sound like the American Dream incarnate. They have in fact checked off every box on what scholars from the American Enterprise Institute have termed the "Millennial Success Sequence" for financial prosperity – get at least a high school education, marry before having children, and acquire full-time work.[27]

Then they had their first kid.

With the arrival of their beloved daughter, stress levels went through the roof, and the Tangs now face a future full of uncertainties.

The Tang's five-month-old infant attends home-based childcare 35+ hours a week, for which the couple pays at least $1,500 a month. This expense, plus the relatively high cost-of-living in the D.C. area, means that they are forced to be renters for the foreseeable future, and distant outlays like college or even orthodontia create a constant low thrum of anxiety.

Carey muses that, "since my job – which thankfully I love! – is the stable money-maker, my career options are constrained, and it's a burden that I am very aware of. I simply cannot lose my job or pursue a position that wouldn't make as much, even if it afforded me other benefits – like more time with my kid." For Yuan, since even talented chefs aren't particularly well-paid, "his only option to not being a stay-at-home parent is for our own restaurant to be successful. If it isn't, he'll stay at home since we can't afford childcare long-term with just my income. And while he's a very active, involved, and invested parent, he wants to work and pursue his own career, too."

Fundamentally, she adds, "the lack of choice is frustrating."

Choice, after all, is what the American value of freedom is all about. Freedom is what you're supposed to be rewarded with for following the success sequence. Freedom to find a job that creates the work-life balance you desire, freedom to pursue the dream of launching one's own business with all of the positive effects that has on the local community and economy, freedom to try something else if that doesn't work out.

Childcare costs can be a freedom killer.

* * *

3,000 miles away in the San Francisco Bay Area, Marie and Nick Baker (not their real names) should be breathing easy. Marie is a licensed child therapist while Nick does software sales. Together, they pull down a combined salary of around $150,000 a year.

After being married for over a decade, the 34-year-olds had a son, John, who is now two years old. Since the couple's ever-changing schedules don't mesh well with the hours of a center- or home-based care, John receives care from a nanny roughly 25 hours a week, at a cost of $2,500 a month. The (very) relative "affordability" of this option was a major factor in the couple taking on a brutal commute by moving from San Francisco proper to the slightly less pricey North Bay. Still, Nick says, "We have to be a working household to keep up largely with the expenses of childcare. It is the number one factor holding us back from being able to do all those bigger adult things you do to 'level up' in life. Continuing education, career development, investing, owning a house…" A pause. "Even now, I can feel the panic setting in because I don't know what to do here."

Nick adds, "It is a huge struggle on a month to month basis to clear checks. Credit card debt seems to mount as we'll tell ourselves that eventually, we'll get on top of the whole situation. But whatever that future solution is that will help us 'get on top' of the situation, it's not here now. There is no safety net. This is what keeps me up at night."

The Bakers have also completed the so-called success sequence. A household income of $150,000 makes most people drool, even in one of the most expensive cities in America. Yet the way Nick talks is the way that we envision a poor family down on their luck talks.

What does that $2,500 a month represent to them? Nick remarks, "They say the happiest raise or promotion in a person's life is the one that gives them financial independence." Not having to pay for childcare "would feel like that."

*　　*　　*

It's not just middle-class families in major metro (or Democratic) areas that are hit hard by the childcare crisis. Julie and Allen Harper (not their real names) live in Asheville, North Carolina, a smallish city of 90,000 with a cost-of-living index close to the national average, nestled in the mountains of a state that has voted Republican in nine of the past ten Presidential elections. The overview of their story may sound familiar: Married and employed, Julie works in education, while Allen is a licensed architect. They have two children, aged five and two; the five-year-old missed the kindergarten age cut-off, so is still in private care until next fall. The older child attends a center-based preschool while the younger is with a home-based provider. Care for the two totals $2,000 a month.

Julie told me over email, "We live paycheck to paycheck because of childcare costs. We live on a very strict budget (down to dollar). Childcare is about one-half of my monthly gross income – it's really unbelievable. If I were to lose my job I know that I would have to pull both of my kids from school immediately because there is no way that I could pay for tuition – this, of course, causes deep stress."

She adds, "I just can't even imagine how our lives would be impacted by having $2,000 a month back. Mostly an ability to sleep easier and enjoy being with my children more. A retirement plan for my husband, investing in our community, philanthropy, savings, more ability to help with our aging parents. But really – just the peace of mind by having savings. I really have felt consumed by the cost of childcare since becoming pregnant at 25 and being the breadwinner of our family for the majority of motherhood. I've totally washed away the dream of having one more child. We can barely afford the two children we have and I live in fear of something happening with our health. I've been so very fortunate – I am grateful for all we have. It feels lucky – which is truly heartbreaking to write."

Fortunate to live on the edge. This is the reality of the American middle class with children under five.

*   *   *

I tell these stories not because the Tangs or Bakers or Harpers are the faces of the childcare crisis – unquestionably, this hits low-income and lower-middle-income families exponentially harder.* Instead, I'm making the intentional choice to illustrate the sheer breadth of the problem; the fact that the childcare pain point has now penetrated the middle class, and in many cases even the upper-middle class, should throw the crisis into sharp relief. In big cities and small towns, red states and blue, on the coasts and in the heartland, childcare costs are straining and at times breaking the backs of the vast majority of young families. When it comes to poorer parents, you unfortunately don't have to go far for examples of how the crisis is crushing the very breath out of them.

For instance, the advocacy group Moms Rising has compiled a document simply titled "Stories of the Childcare Struggle in America," with dozens of vignettes. A typical story reads like this one from a Pennsylvania woman named Melissa: "I am currently a single mother in the middle of a divorce and cannot find affordable, acceptable childcare to allow me to re-enter the workforce. To work a minimum wage job and pay $10/hour childcare, just doesn't make any sense. The problem this is

---

* For a poignant illustration of how childcare intersects with poverty, and the inadequacy of the systems we have in place for helping low-income families, I recommend Stephanie Land's memoir *Maid*. As Land explained on Twitter, "My daughter took her first steps on that dirty, tiled floor of a homeless shelter because I'd just escaped an abusive relationship with a couple hundred dollars. Because my family couldn't help us. Because I simply couldn't find a job. Since I couldn't find work, a grant for childcare wasn't obtainable. You see, I needed to obtain a job that I could do while my daughter was at daycare before I'd get approved for that grant. What was I supposed to do with my kid between finding work and being approved?" I have heard variations of this story many, many times, including that of one woman who was finally approved for a childcare subsidy on the same day she was fired from her recently-found job because childcare problems had caused her to miss a shift.

creating is I am going quickly in debt. My income-to-debt ratio is way out of whack, and I am creating all kinds of financial issues."[28]

There are also a huge number of struggling, largely-ignored families who fall between the poverty line and the self-sufficiency line, which is when you can cover basic needs without assistance. These are families that make too much to be eligible for even the meager subsidies that currently exist – and who don't qualify for Head Start, etc. – but who are an income ladder rung below the families we've met. The United Way uses the somewhat awkward acronym ALICE to describe these families: Asset Limited, Income Constrained, Employed.[29] In other words, these families have very little wealth (they probably rent their house and finance their cars), their income is entirely consumed by expenses (they have little-to-no savings or ability to make investments), and all available workers in the household are employed.

There are a *lot* of ALICE families, and in fact significantly more ALICE families than families below the poverty line. Take, for instance, a state very different than the ones thus far mentioned: Idaho. In 2016, the federal poverty line in Idaho for a family of four was $24,300. The self-sufficiency survival line for a family of four with a four-year-old and an infant was $53,664. Every family of four with young kids who brought in between $24,300 and $53,664 are considered ALICE families. Whereas 16 percent of all Idaho households fell below the poverty line that year, another one-in-four – 26 percent! – were in the ALICE range[*].

Even more than my squarely middle-class peers, young ALICE families cannot get ahead. Why? You guessed it: childcare costs. A full 20 percent of that survival budget is dedicated to childcare, and it's the single largest line-item, quite a lot more than housing or food in low-cost Idaho. One would need to make the equivalent of nearly $27 an hour to meet the self-sufficiency threshold; take out the childcare component, and it's closer to $20 an hour (and, if one were making anything between $20 and $27 an hour, suddenly those extra dollars just got freed up, and income got less constrained, which can lead to assets getting less limited).

Consider 100 young families in an average state who utilize non-parental care. About fifteen live below the poverty line. The lack of reliable, affordable childcare is preventing them from holding down

---

[*] To be clear, the 16 percent and 26 percent numbers include all households, not just families with kids

gainful, upwardly-mobile employment. Another quarter are ALICE families. Childcare costs are keeping them stuck running in place, sweat building up. Of the remaining 60, the majority are the cash-poor middle class for whom childcare costs are causing stress, sacrifice, and financial fragility. What's more, these numbers don't include families with a stay-at-home parent, who, as we'll see later in this section, are also flailing despite not regularly paying for outside care.

There's a reason that half of all Millennials – today's and tomorrow's parents – consider the American Dream to be "dead."[30]

And none of this has begun to touch on the essential question of the quality of care, which, as we know, only shapes the literal wiring of children's brains.

How, oh how, did we get here?

*   *   *

The History of American Childcare

The history and trajectory of American childcare lays on four evolving pillars, summarized in the compass that opened this section: the role of women in society; our understanding of early childhood development; the number of dual-worker households; and costs of care.

Until very recently, child-rearing during the earliest years was seen as purely women's work. Even today, surveys reveal that while the public has gotten used to women working outside the home, they still think an ideal situation is one in which the mother is significantly involved in childcare. In a 2013 Pew survey, fully half of the respondents said children are "better off" when their mother stays home, while less than 10 percent said the same about stay-at-home fathers.[31] Historian Sonya Michel, who literally wrote the book on American childcare history, has shown that in the 18th, 19th, and early 20th centuries, separating mother from child and child from mother was considered an absolute negative.[32]

Formalized childcare in America began to develop in the second half of the 19th century as a reluctant response to the fact that low-income mothers had no choice but to find work*. Before that, if you needed

---

* Prior to this time, the question of childcare was largely a moot point, as the vast majority of early Americans were farmers living on multigenerational farms.

childcare and were rich, you hired (or enslaved) a caretaker; if you were poor (or a slave[*]) you found a friend or relative to watch your little ones, literally left them by themselves all day, or figured out a way to take them to work with you, danger or no.[33] Starting around the 1850s, a small number of "day nurseries" were started by charitable organizations as safe holding places for the young children of poor working mothers. However, these were few, scattered, and utterly unregulated.

As the dawn of the 20th century approached, New York philanthropist Josephine Jewell Dodge and her compatriots made moves to popularize childcare. They put together a widely-attended Model Day Nursery at the 1893 Chicago World's Fair, and five years later launched the National Federation of Day Nurseries[†].[34]

Yet the idea was slow to catch on. With society preferring to keep mothers at home with their children, what public monies were set aside went mainly to "mother's pensions," small stipends for poor or widowed mothers with the goal of alleviating their need to work. Emphasizing pensions over care, as Michel puts it, pushed childcare "further into the shadows of charity" and away from the light of a common good or a universal right. By 1916, there were only around 700 day nurseries in the entire country – versus over 250,000 public schools – and most were of awful quality[§]. One paper describes the day nurseries thusly: "They were crowded, marginally funded, staffed by untrained personnel, and barely able to meet minimal standards of sanitation."[35] One beleaguered woman might be found caring for 30 or more young children.

Starting in the 1920s, a distinct set of early pre-K programs, known (confusingly) as "nursery schools" began to emerge. In explicit contrast

---

[*] On larger plantations, older and infirm slaves (as well as children not yet able to work the fields) were often made to watch over as many as 100 young children. There are other reports of enslaved mothers forced to simply strap their babies to their already straining backs.

[†] Dodge's dominant leadership of the NFDN is important because it was the primary voice for childcare in the first third of the 20th century, and it was a decidedly problematic one. Dodge herself was opposed to women's suffrage, and the NFDN by policy excluded Blacks. That a group of wealthy white women with these types of views had this level of influence for that long helps explain why a movement for universal childcare remained nonexistent in the U.S.

[§] Today we have around 100,000 public schools. The heightened number of schools during this era was due to the continued prevalence of one-room schoolhouses.

to ill-regarded day nurseries, these nursery schools were more 'educationally-focused,' had college-educated staff, and were targeted towards middle-class families who could pay a fee. Though they had their critics, nursery schools got around society's frowning because children were only attending a few hours a day while their mothers – who were not employed outside the home – took a class on the latest parenting fad or did something else considered an appropriate, socially beneficial activity*. This artificial distinction between early childhood education and childcare, emerging along class lines, is still with us today; however, neither was considered a common good worthy of significant public investment, and neither took off: by 1932 there were only 500 nursery schools nationwide.[36]

It wasn't until women were desperately needed in the workforce that public, government-funded childcare became a reality. During World War II, as women rushed in to fill the jobs of men deploying overseas, Congress passed the Lantham Act, which allocated public funding for, among other things, childcare centers. However, there was still deep discomfort with the idea of widespread maternal employment, and as soon as the war ended, the funding was pulled.

Nevertheless, the train of women in the workforce had left the station; the years after WWII began the steady growth of a tumbledown patchwork of formal and informal childcare providers that created the contours of today's landscape†. The closest that America got to full government-funded childcare was the 1971 Comprehensive Child Development Act.[37] This bipartisan effort to establish public childcares with sliding-scale fees (not identical to, but not that dissimilar from, public schools) made it all the way to the desk of President Richard Nixon, who summarily vetoed it. It's fascinating to read the rationale that Congress wrote into the Act because it shows that the leaders of our land have in large part already set down the case I'm trying to make today. The legislation stated that Congress had found:

---

* Also, in an impressive feat of paternalism, nursery schools were pitched as a way of preparing the well-heeled young women who taught in them for their future lives as mothers and homemakers.
† This period is broadly known by academics as the "Second Demographic Transition" where post-WWII changes like rapidly increasing wealth, rapidly decreasing prices of goods, and arrival of the birth control pill significantly changed family structures and women's options.

"(1) millions of American children are suffering unnecessary harm from the lack of adequate child development services, particularly during early childhood years;

(2) comprehensive child development programs, including a full range of health, education, and social services, are essential to the achievement of the full potential of America's children and should be available **as a matter of right** to all children regardless of economic, social, and family background; (emphasis mine)

(3) children with special needs must receive full and special consideration in planning any child development programs and, pending the availability of such programs for all children, priority must be given to preschool children with the greatest economic and social need;

(4) while no mother may be forced to work outside the home as a condition for using child development programs, such programs are essential to allow many parents to undertake or continue full- or part-time employment, training, or education; and,

(5) it is essential that the planning and operation of such programs be undertaken as a partnership of parents, community, and local government."[38]

Despite this remarkably forward-thinking preamble, the defeat of the 1971 bill saw childcare kicked all the way back to the bottom of the public policy mountain; Nixon wasn't going to budge, and the 1973 economic recession squashed any momentum towards increased government spending. The moment had passed. Since then, there's been no equivalently bold summit attempt, and federal government policy towards childcare has mainly revolved around modest subsidy schemes for low-income families and modest tax breaks for everyone else. While state public pre-K programs have created a decent number of slots for four- and in some cases three-year-olds, no state or city has anything approaching a comprehensive system of care for kids birth-through-five.

Two connecting threads of this story stand out: First, childcare's long history of being put at the feet of mothers means it has not been considered in the jurisdiction of government. Why did Nixon veto that bill? Because, he wrote in his veto statement, it "would be truly a long leap into the dark for the United States Government and the American people ... plung[ing] headlong financially into supporting child development would commit the vast moral authority of the National Government to the side of communal approaches to child rearing over [and] against the family-centered approach."[39]

Nixon, spurred on by conservative religious advisors like Pat Robertson, wrote that the idea was "radical."[*] As law professor Meredith Harbach has written, even in case law, "privacy and nonintervention norms have both reflected and reinforced the idea that childcare is a private matter, involving private prerogatives, provided in the private home, and a matter of private responsibility. These norms animated historical debates over the proper state role in childcare, and continue to influence them today."[40]

Second, the negative stance towards mothers working was held up with the backing of junk science. These theories suggested that young children required full-time maternal care in order to develop in a healthy fashion, and that no other caregiving setup could accomplish this goal.[41] Thus, the thinking went, women and children were literally damaged by being thrust apart[†].

It's important to understand just how epically, tragically wrong conventional wisdom has often been about child development, and just how seriously these incorrect conclusions were taken by parents and broader society. For instance, the U.S. Department of Labor's former Children's Bureau put out extremely popular "Infant Bulletins" that *literally said parents shouldn't play with their babies.* "The rule that

---

[*] Author Gail Collins notes in her book *When Everything Changed* that the veto statement was intentionally hardline because "The goal was not just to kill the bill but also to bury the idea of a national child-care entitlement forever."

[†] Children during this time were largely seen as tiny adults who, depending on their environment, would take one of two predetermined developmental paths: healthy or pathological. The term "child psychiatry" wasn't used in America until 1935, to give you a sense of how long it took to even start considering children on their own terms.

parents should not play with the baby may seem hard," the 1914 *Bulletin* reads (again, this is the official message of the United States government!), "but it is without a doubt a safe one. A young, delicate, or nervous baby especially needs rest and quiet, and however robust the child, much of the play that is indulged in is more or less harmful."[*42]

Given this, it shouldn't surprise you to learn that conventional wisdom was also horridly off about the effects of women working. So-called child experts like Douglas Thom warned in the 1920s about "worn and weary" working mothers unable to provide good care for their children; working mothers were seen as nothing less than psychologically unhealthy.[43] Even beloved Dr. Benjamin Spock, as late as the 1958 edition of *Baby and Childcare*, wrote that "good mother care during the earliest childhood is the surest way to produce [useful and well-adjusted citizens]. It doesn't make sense to let mothers go to work making dresses or tapping typewriters in an office and have them pay other people to do a poorer job of bringing up their own children ... a day nursery or a 'baby farm' is no good for an infant."[†44]

It wasn't until the 1960s and 70s – right around when the groundwork for the Comprehensive Child Development Act was being laid – that the combined weight of work done by psychologists Harry Harlow, Jean Piaget, John Bowlby, Mary Ainsworth, and others would finally realign the consensus on child development. These efforts cemented once and for all that children's minds and development are distinct from adults, that children need loving and responsive caregiving to grow emotionally and cognitively, and – perhaps most importantly for our purposes – that children can develop healthily in many different caregiving circumstances.[45] Since then, our grasp on child development has ascended by an ongoing series of leaps and bounds, propelled by a proliferation of child-focused research centers and previously

---

[*] There were a few visionaries who grasped early on what young children were really capable of and what they actually needed – Maria Montessori was operating schools in Italy in the 1900s and 1910s – but it would be many decades before ideas like hers caught fire in the U.S. For more on the fraught history of American child-rearing advice, I recommend Ann Hulbert's book *Raising America: Experts, Parents, and a Century of Advice About Children*.
[†] In reality, of course, babies can bond with multiple primary caregivers (including, surprise, the father!), requiring strong attachment to at least one for healthy development. Moreover, secure attachments are durable. It probably doesn't need to be said, but just to be safe: An attentive mother who happens to work during the day does no harm whatsoever to herself or her children.

unthinkable advances in technology.

So while it's hard to remember in this era of supposed gender equality and fMRI machines that can trace week-by-week fetal brain development, for the vast majority of America's history, the idea of government providing free childcare like free public education *was* radical – indeed, it was nonsensical.

*   *   *

Two additional developments over the past half-century add color to our current crisis.

The first is the increasing need for two-earner households as the cost of living rises and wages stagnate. In 1960, only a quarter of married American households had both adults working; by 2010, it was fully 60 percent.[46] While plenty of this shift was a welcome result of women's increasing choices, many times it was a matter of necessity; today, half of working middle-class women are their families' primary breadwinners, including Carey and Julie. During this time period, big-ticket costs – college, homes, health care – all skyrocketed, and they only continue to climb. There has also been a corresponding rise in household debt as student loans pile up, mortgages balloon, and medical bills get dumped onto credit cards.[47] Yet despite these modern realities, glacial wage growth means the purchasing power of today's average worker is roughly equivalent to that of the average worker in the 1970s.[48]

This rise in dual-worker households – both forced and voluntary – of course has the effect of meaning that millions more families require non-parental childcare. The same is true to an even greater extreme for single parents, around three-quarters of whom are currently in the workforce.

The other development is the rising cost of outside care. Childcare costs have been going up at *triple* the average rate of all consumer goods.[49] Since we know that extra money isn't going to raising teacher wages, why the growing expense? The answers seem to lie in two places: rising real estate prices, and an increased demand for safety and quality.

The first is straightforward: particularly in urban areas, as cities have their new heyday, rents are on the rise. This is having major consequences for affordable residential housing but also for affordable commercial real estate (which, for home-based care providers, is one in the same). Since most childcare providers operate on razor-thin margins, they can't absorb a rent increase without raising their rates to compensate[*].

The growing safety and quality expenses are a bit more nuanced. Although horrific incidents of abuse or death in childcare settings are exceedingly rare, they make headlines, and they've led to demands for government regulation. These regulations tend to focus on (mostly defensible, sometimes banal) checkbox items – fingerprint background checks for all the teachers, ensuring an entryway that meets a minimum fire code width, playgrounds with a proper amount of cushioning ground cover, etc. Coming into compliance with an ever-increasing raft of health and safety regulations is expensive.[50]

Similarly, as more states and the federal government have made a laudable attempt to focus on the quality of childcare, costs further stack up. In order to be eligible to accept public subsidy dollars, a center may be required to ensure all of its teachers receive a certain number of training hours; but since those training hours must happen outside normal work hours, teachers need to be compensated. Similarly, to move up levels in a state's quality-rating system, a provider may need to purchase one of a menu of verified high-quality curricula. Again, that's something we should want, but it's also something that costs money the provider doesn't have. There's no choice but to raise rates.

So why isn't childcare free for families, despite more parents needing care and the costs of care exploding? Because of a (non-)system of care that developed haphazardly and with little public support. Because of a society that is just starting to come around to the fact that the earliest years are critical for brain development, and that infants and toddlers have a rich cognitive and emotional life. Perhaps more than anything, because of a society that has historically had – and continues to wrestle with – a deep-rooted discomfort with mothers working outside the home.

*   *   *

---

[*] Really, providers can't currently absorb *any* fixed cost increases. When the nonprofit Child Care Aware of Washington State surveyed providers about how they would handle the state's (welcome!) minimum wage increase, 72 percent said they'd have to raise rates for families.

The Contrasting History of American Public K-12 Education

The contrasting history of public K-12 education in America is important to understand if we are to apply the same underlying philosophy to childcare. That said, we'll take this story in more concise, broad sweeps, as the details matter a bit less.

The rise of mass, free public schooling (grades 1 through 8) happened in the early-to-mid-1800s. Prior to that, there had been fits and starts – Massachusetts and Virginia were early adopters – but never a true movement. Those initial spurts of common schooling came out of a desire to either educate children so they would be of good moral character or, in the not entirely comforting words of Thomas Jefferson, so that a small number of brilliant people might rise to defend democracy in the next generation:

"The indigence of the greater number disabling them from so educating, at their own expense, those of their children whom nature hath fitly formed and disposed to become useful instruments for the public." Thomas Jefferson wrote this statement in the preamble to his *Bill for the General Diffusion of Knowledge*, "it is better that such should be sought for and educated at the common expense of all, than that the happiness of all should be confided to the weak or wicked."

When common schools did explode, it was a coalition of these types of more idealistic virtues and simple economic realities – again, volcanic pressure – that carried the day. Starting in 1820, and over the next half-century, towns and cities began to fill up as the forerunners to today's agribusiness consumed small family farms. Simultaneously, there was a major wave of immigration driven by events such as the Irish Potato Famine.[51] There needed to be somewhere to shape these crowds of children into citizens and workers. There needed to be somewhere for them to go and be kept out of trouble during the day. Those interested in worker's rights needed a place where the youth could gain skills that would allow them to get ahead in life. Horace Mann, the so-called 'father of common schools,' tried to bring all of these threads together. As one scholar puts it, quoting historian Lawrence Cremin:

"Mann's commitment to common schools stemmed from his belief that political stability and social harmony depended on universal education ... His message to the working classes was the promise that 'education … is the great equalizer of the conditions of men, the balance wheel of the social machinery.' To men of property, he asserted that their security and prosperity depended upon having literate and law-abiding neighbors who were competent workers and who would, via the common school, learn of the sanctity of private property. To all, he proclaimed that Providence had decreed that education was the '*absolute right* of every human being that comes into the world.'"[52] (emphasis Cremin's)

Unsurprisingly, there was serious opposition to the idea of common schools (and also unsurprisingly, 'universal' education turned out to be much more universal when one was white and male; many Southern states were also spending the mid-1800s passing laws making it illegal to teach a slave to read). The rich didn't all love the idea of being taxed; the Catholic church didn't love the idea of secular education, and some business magnates didn't love the idea of workers getting thoughts of things like 'rights' into their heads. Still, on the whole, Protestant progressives, captains of industry, and early labor unions ("workingmen's parties") were in a rare alignment, and enough states adopted common schools that it forced the hand of the others. In 1852, Mann's state of Massachusetts passed the first compulsory schooling law, though, by that time, many historians think it was *fait accompli* – the laws "lagged, rather than led" the spike in enrollment.[53]

Mass common schooling put education squarely in the realm of government, and educational administration and bureaucracy began to grow like kudzu around the scaffolding of the schools. An inviolable right (for some) to access a free public education – and government's obligation to provide it – started to be written into state constitutions. Public education became an entitlement, one we don't even think twice about today. A move towards centralization accompanied the continued growth of cities at the turn of the 20th century (in stark contrast with childcare being thrust "further into the shadows of charity" during this time period). There began a ceaseless and ongoing search for what historian David Tyack termed the "One Best System" of education.[54]

The 20th century can fly by in a blur for our purposes: the High School Movement from 1910-1940 – again, business interests plus a Progressive Era disdain for child labor – the GI Bill, Brown v. Board of Education, and eventually the 1965 Elementary and Secondary Education Act (ESEA), a signature piece of President Johnson's War on

Poverty which brought the federal government onto the education field (Head Start also came in this package, again as a foray into helping poor children). ESEA launched a truly epic increase in educational investments, from about 3 percent of gross domestic product (GDP) to 6 percent of GDP, to the point that combined federal, state, and local spending on education is now over $670 billion a year. By comparison, federal spending on childcare subsidies through the Child Care and Development Fund, the dominant source of public childcare investment, is about $7 billion a year*.[55] Next up was the 1983 *A Nation at Risk* report, which put educational quality front and center, though with concerns that echoed back to the mid-1800s: America wasn't producing enough skilled workers, leading to fears of both falling behind economically and promoting crime and delinquency.

The final relevant note of this history is the relatively recent expansion of first Kindergarten and then pre-K for 4-year-olds and in a few cases 3-year-olds. Generally, this has been pitched as a way to help level the academic playing field for lower-income children, harkening back to childcare's roots in charity. For instance, in Rhode Island Gov. Gina Raimondo's 2019 State of the State Address announcing a proposal for universal pre-K, she focused not on the expansion of a common good but on the fact that "we know that kids who go to high-quality preschool are more likely to graduate high school, more likely to get a good job and keep a good job, and less likely to commit a crime."[56]

Again, two threads stick out.

First, nowhere in the history of public education is the role of mothers in child-rearing particularly prominent, save for issues around the teaching profession†. Despite a strong preference for maternal care in the early years, society has clearly decided that once a child reaches a certain age, maternal linkage is no longer critical. In the 19th century, that was somewhere around age 6 or 7. Today, we seem happy enough with putting that line at age 4, and we're getting increasingly OK with age 3. The infant and toddler years remain more contentious, at least for

---

* To put this in an international context, data from the Organization for Economic Cooperation and Development (OECD) shows that among 34 developed nations, the U.S. is currently above-average in public education spending as a percentage of GDP; in spending on early care and education, we rank second-to-last.

† Through much of the first half of the 20th century, a female teacher was forced to resign upon becoming pregnant.

the moment.

Second, the business class has been the key driver behind the expansion of free public education, yet until literally the past few years, business hasn't touched childcare. While the democratic ideals are all well and good, they have never been enough to move the needle on their own. Business wanted competent laborers, so we gave them primary schools. Business wanted factory workers for their assembly lines, so we gave them high schools. Business wanted problem solvers, so we gave them colleges and universities. In the past two decades, business has realized that the first period of life has an overwhelming impact on a child's trajectory, and so we're giving them pre-K. For better or worse, business is going to be a major player in establishing a birth-to-five system.

*   *   *

Learning From History to Inform Our Future

One point should be made plainly: In my view, childcare should be treated like K-12 public education, but it should not *be* K-12 public education. America's public education system serves over 50 million youth and is by its very nature forced into averages; historian Carl Kaestle (no relation to the late, great NPR host) once described American education as "a gigantic standardized compromise most of us have learned to live with."[57] There are many, many problems with our public education system, from inadequately compensated teachers, resource and rigor inequities along racial and socioeconomic lines, and regulation that is at turns too prescriptive and too laissez-faire. No one founding a new country would look at the U.S. education system and think, "copy-paste." And, as we'll detail later, 'common childcares,' a la common schools – they do exist in some nations – are a questionable solution here, for reasons both political and practical.

However.

Our education system has one underlying precept that is vitally important: *Education in America is seen as a common good.* It is considered a proper area for governmental (departments of education, etc.), democratic (school boards, etc.), and societal (PTAs, tutoring programs, etc.) action[*]. Since it is a common good, it is, therefore, a recipient of what Jefferson termed the "common expense," putting schools in the same taxpayer-funded category as national defense, parks, or fire departments[†]. The average per-pupil expenditure in 2016 was $11,762, with substantial state-by-state variation – New York led the pack at $22,366 per student.[58]

While history allows us to understand why childcare has not to date been considered a common good, that stance no longer holds up to scrutiny. For all but the most affluent, our modern families cannot sustainably absorb the costs of care without major disruption to their ability to contribute economically. Our grasp of early childhood development has taken a quantum leap, and we now know the extent to which brain development is influenced by high-quality early experiences as well as family financial stability. Most importantly, our society's ideas about women getting to choose whether they work outside the home have evolved[‡]. Childcare should be free *because childcare should be considered a common good*. In fact, if you support the idea of free, universal K-12 schooling, it is now nonsensical to do anything but support the idea of free, universal birth-to-five childcare.

The business community seems to be just coming around to this view, which bodes well for adoption of the sort of proposals laid forth in this book. In 2017, the U.S. Chamber of Commerce Foundation released a report entitled *Workforce of Today, Workforce of Tomorrow: The Business Case for High-Quality Childcare*.[59] Written by Katharine B. Stevens of the American Enterprise Institute, it's a remarkable document in its authorship, its forthrightness, and because it directly applies the common-school philosophy to childcare. As such, it's worth quoting at some length:

---

[*] The preferred extent of this intervention is of course up for debate, as some want the federal Department of Education abolished, others want appointed over elected school boards, and so on.

[†] The technical Economics definition of a common or public good is a good that is "non-rivalrous" and "non-excludable." Non-rivalrous means that one person's usage of the good doesn't diminish the ability of another person to use it. Non-excludable means that it's almost impossible to stop someone from using the good. There are varying "purity" levels of public goods (arguably, if the fire department is putting out a fire at your house, they might be slower getting to my house), but primary and secondary education has long been considered to fit within the category.

[‡] This is quantifiable: In a 2012 Pew survey, only 18 percent of respondents said that women "should return to their traditional role in society."

"One root of [the problem of not having enough high-skilled workers for today's economy] is that we've underestimated the importance of the earliest years of life. For most of history, the essential early foundation for all subsequent learning and development was laid largely in the home. But today, an unprecedented number of American mothers are in the workforce, and millions of young children are in paid childcare for a substantial portion of their early years. And while childcare is a necessary support for working parents, it also has a critical impact on children during the most consequential phase of human development.

Research shows that starting at birth, young children are continuously and rapidly learning — wherever they are, and from whomever they're with. Indeed, the commonly made distinction between 'care' and 'education' in early childhood is a false one. Childcare *is* early education, regardless of the building it occurs in or what we call it. The question is only whether it's advancing or impeding children's learning.

...In fact, childcare is unique among early childhood programs because, if done right, it can serve two crucial purposes simultaneously: ensuring the healthy development of young children while enabling their parents to contribute as productive members of the workforce. By laying the crucial groundwork for tomorrow's workforce and supporting a strong workforce today, high-quality childcare builds our nation's human capital two generations at a time."

Unfortunately, the Chamber's report walks right up to the natural, logical line of making childcare universal and free for families, then stops short. The recommendations include laudable acts like having business vocally support high-quality early care through op-eds and the such; adopting family-friendly policies in the workplace like a childcare fringe benefit or even an on-site childcare center; and working with coalitions of nonprofits, government, and other stakeholders to improve local childcare quality. None of these recommendations, you will notice, addresses the fundamental structural fault line of there not being enough money in the system despite parents being unable to bear the current level of costs.

Indeed, there's one final piece of the case for free childcare that we have not yet talked about, which is that putting more money in the pockets of families has a *direct* positive impact on student's later academic and life achievement.[60] The reasons are hopefully obvious by now: increasing family income reduces family stress, and a family that is not chronically stressed is the soil upon which optimal brain development flowers.

The effects here are tremendously large for even relatively modest increases in family income, and there's an outsized impact on lower-income families*. Just adding a couple thousand dollars to a cash-strapped family's income gets you close to the student achievement boost of switching out a mediocre teacher for an excellent teacher.[61] A recent landmark report by the National Academies of Sciences, *A Roadmap to Reducing Child Poverty*, put it bluntly: "Many programs that alleviate poverty – either directly, by providing income transfers, or indirectly, by providing food, housing, or medical care – have been shown to improve child well-being."[62] The policy the interdisciplinary panel of experts found could have the single largest impact moving forward? Give families money. In fact, financial security is so tightly tied to child outcomes that the Centers for Disease Control lists "strengthen economic supports to families" as one of the five key strategies for preventing child abuse and neglect.[63]

Given everything we've reviewed in this chapter – given the stories of the Tangs and Bakers and Harpers and the millions of struggling middle-class families and ALICE families and families in poverty around the country – imagine the impact of granting families the equivalent of $15,000 a year or more across the board. All while allowing parents to work and improving the quality of children's earliest, most critical experiences.

Childcare should be a common good. Childcare should be an unconditional right. Childcare should be free for families.

---

* Researchers have clever ways of testing this through natural experiments: looking at families on either side of the eligibility cut-off for the Earned Income Tax Credit, looking at families who were paid for choosing to allow natural gas fracking rights on their land, looking at Native American families that got payouts from newly opened casinos, etc.

Chapter 2: The Many Faces – and Brains – of Childcare

Who's Minding the Kids?

A professor of mine once started a lecture with the simple instruction to imagine a tree. Where is that specific tree, he asked, referring to the picture in our mind's eye. Can you take me to it? The answer, of course, is that when most of us envision a tree, we actually envision some archetype we have in our head: an imaginary, average, quintessential tree, probably existing in springtime with a thick trunk and bushy green leaves[*]. Similarly, if I ask you to imagine a teacher or a doctor or children playing, we'll all end up with a relatively similar picture even if the specifics differ – the blackboard, the scrubs, the playground.

Ask people to envision childcare, though, and you'll get wildly different answers. For some people, it's a mom pushing a stroller down a park path. For others, it's smiling grandparents bouncing a baby on their knee. Many think of a classroom full of boisterous toddlers, or perhaps a nanny reading a book to a child while the parents get ready for work.

Childcare is not one thing, and that's critical context when developing a new system. Nor, as we'll talk about in this chapter, is one childcare setting inherently better or worse than another.

First, though, we need to set some common definitions for when we think about how Child Development Credits would work. These definitions are my own synthesis of several governmental and trade groups' definitions because I don't think any single current set of definitions is particularly useful for the general public.

"Formal care" is group childcare provided in a building other than a person's home. These are your centers, your religiously-based childcares (churches, Jewish community centers), your Head Starts and pre-Ks

---

[*] If you were born and raised in America, that is; there are, of course, cultural differences at play (and maybe Arizonans would imagine a cactus instead?)

provided by public schools or states[*]. Formal settings usually have classrooms split up by age groups, with a fairly high number of children in a classroom based on legal maximum child-to-adult ratios. There may be, for instance, 16 three-year-olds and two teachers in one room. Formal settings are much more likely to have teachers with professional degrees and certifications, and they are much more likely to be licensed by the state; that said, as Section II will illuminate, quality varies tremendously. These programs tend to operate on standardized schedules – a common one is 7:00am-6:00pm, Monday-Friday, although school-based programs often close much earlier. There is, however, a recent rise in 24-hour and weekend formal providers (what author Alissa Quart calls "extreme daycare"). Formal care is, with the exception of 1:1 nannies, generally the most expensive form of care.

"Informal care" (sometimes called "family childcare" or "home-based care") is small-group or individual care provided in a home for which a fee is paid. The classic informal care provider is one adult who hosts a few non-related children in her home – "family childcare" in this case refers to the care being provided in the home of another family, in contrast to a center or other formal care location. Informal care also includes nannies and au pairs that provide care in the child's own home. Informal care providers tend to be much more lightly regulated than formal providers. Most states do not require informal providers to register their business until they are caring for a minimum number of children, often four to six (although in South Dakota you can legally care for 12(!) children without notifying the state). Informal providers may cater to more specialized populations, such as families who only speak a given language.

"Friend, family & neighbor (FFN) care" (sometimes called "kith and

---

[*] Pre-Kindergarten, for what it's worth, is a rather arbitrary term with its roots in the divergent histories of the middle class-focused "nursery schools" vs. poor-focused "day nurseries". A four-year-old in a home-based care or in parental care isn't *not* being prepared for Kindergarten, and the same goes for infants and toddlers. The whole idea that pre-K is distinct from the rest of the birth-to-five sector is a sign of the backwards way America tends to look at early childhood; more on this later in the chapter.

kin care") is individual or sibling care provided for free by a relative, friend, or neighbor*. A grandmother who cares daily for her grandchildren is the archetype here. FFN care can be considered a subset of informal care – the care occurs in a home – though the lack of cost and importance of relational networks makes it distinct. For all intents and purposes, FFN care is completely unregulated.

"Parental care," of course, is full-time care provided by a parent or legal guardian.

Lastly, there's something researchers call "no regular arrangement" care, which means the child has, well, no regular arrangement. This usually involves a patchwork of parental care, informal care, and FFN care. The care arrangement may change week to week or month to month based upon availability of caregivers (driven by a parent's shift schedule at work, for example), the funds to pay for outside care, and so on.

*   *   *

So, given those buckets, where does care happen in America? Despite all the perfectly reasonable energy, money, and research paper ink spent on formal care, the vast majority of young children receive informal, FFN, or parental care.[64]

(Each block represents 100,000 children)

---

* In truth, it's for free OR a small fee. While a grandparent may watch the kids for free, it's more likely the neighbor is getting some cash or traded services under the table. Either way, it's by *far* the cheapest and least regulated form of non-parental care.

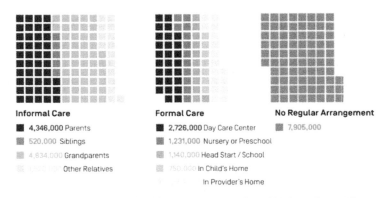

Informal Care

- ■ 4,346,000 Parents
- ▣ 520,000 Siblings
- ▣ 4,634,000 Grandparents
- ▣ Other Relatives

Formal Care

- ■ 2,726,000 Day Care Center
- ▣ 1,231,000 Nursery or Preschool
- ▣ 1,140,000 Head Start / School
- ▣ 750,000 In Child's Home
- In Provider's Home

No Regular Arrangement

- ▣ 7,905,000

Source: Lynda Laughlin, Who's Minding the Kids? Childcare Arrangements: Spring 2011, [Census Bureau, U.S. Department of Commerce, 2013].

As you can see, this graphic, from the think tank New America's excellent *Care Report*, actually undersells the point because it uses different definitions of informal vs. formal care. Only parents and FFN are in their 'informal' bucket; for our purposes, the 2.3 million children in home-based care – 23 shaded blocks from the middle – should be moved to the left. In terms of the sheer number of locations where care is provided, *97 percent* of caregiving settings are homes, not formal buildings.[65]

Just to add to the fun, tremendous variances are hiding in this data depending on how you cut it.[66] For instance, as a child gets older, they're relatively more likely to be in formal care, and relatively less likely to be in parental care (and vice versa). These differences can be quite large*. Significant variation also emerges when you look at families by education level, income level, number of adults in the household, and so on.

The other wrinkle is that many families – about one in five – utilize *multiple* regular care arrangements, and so fit into several categories.[67] We'll meet one such family later in this section. These are families that may, for instance, use formal care for part of the day and then have a relative provide care for a few hours until the parents get home. My own family fits the multiple-use description: my wife cares for our girls three days a week, and they're at a center the other two days.

---

* As one example, slightly less than 50 percent of infants are in an external care arrangement (formal, informal, or FFN), versus nearly three-quarters of 3s and 4s.

None of this is simple nor straightforward. And for all these reasons, childcare is an absolute beast for public policy to get its hands around. It's the imagining-a-tree problem. If you want to impact what happens in higher education, you can zero in on colleges and universities. If you want to impact what happens in medicine, you can zero in on the hospitals and doctor's offices[†]. If you want to impact early childhood, you have to be everywhere at once, with tentacles reaching into places as far-flung as publicly-funded school-based pre-Ks and the sacred privacy of the home.

The only viable option is to flip the question on its head: worry less about the form of care, and more about the people providing the care and the families choosing what care is best for their child.

*   *   *

Quality Matters Far More Than Setting

The good news is that focusing on caregivers – wherever they might be – actually accomplishes society's goal of laying a strong foundation for the next generation. This is a particularly urgent goal since in many states, less than two in three children are arriving at Kindergarten with the literacy, numeracy, social, and behavioral foundations that set them up for success.[68]

Because of how children's brains develop, there is nothing inherently magical about receiving "early education" in any particular setting. While you can find many paeans to the Montessori, Waldorf, or Reggio-Emilia preschool models, or perhaps your sister swears her nanny walks on water, or you come from a family that believes only the mother should be shepherding the young children, the fact is that *children can learn anywhere there is a responsive, loving adult and something to pique their interest.*

As early childhood expert Erika Christakis writes in her vitally important book *The Importance of Being Little*, it almost requires more effort to *stop* young children from learning than to cause it.[69] All kids

---

[†] These are oversimplifications, of course. Both higher education and public health also have a web of factors that influence them. The point, however, is that they have easily identifiable points of entry; childcare does not.

are literally born learners – babies can start mimicking sticking out their tongues while they are mere minutes old. Christakis calls out that "there is a surprisingly fixed, but false, belief that what we call learning must come from somewhere outside of the child, to be given, or withheld, by a qualified adult. But every young child's brain contains the basis for learning. Wherever that child *is* is where we can find the child's curriculum. Some early childhood educators capture this reality in the phrase, 'the child's environment is the curriculum.'"

This truism may be programmed into our species. Grover J. "Russ" Whitehurst, a former senior U.S. Department of Education official, has put forward what he calls the "good enough" model of early childhood. Based on a wide range of research, Whitehurst offers:

"[The 'good enough' model] is an evolutionary perspective that sees the human species as having evolved in circumstances that support normal development of brain and behavior in a wide range of environments, including those in which parents and communities do not invest extraordinary time and attention in the rearing of their young. It posits a floor with respect to early stimulation, the good-enough point, above which the vast majority of children will experience normal development of brain and behavior without the need for special programs or expensive enrichment experiences."[70]

Put another way, since for most of human history parents were busy hunting-gathering or tending crops, it doesn't make a ton of sense that children would need intensive, hyper-curated caregiving in order to thrive[*].

Don't misunderstand – different levels of quality exist in early childhood settings, period. You can easily find a center that is providing a higher-quality experience than another, in turn leading to different outcomes for the children under their care. This is measurable: we will talk in Section II about tools that early childhood professionals use to assess and improve the experience they are providing children. As one rage-inducing illustration of low quality, I recently heard an account of

---

[*] There are, in my opinion, limitations to the "good enough" model – many historical elements of childhood, including sky-high child labor and child mortality rates, thankfully no longer apply. Moreover, both the risk factors and required skills for success that come with growing up in our current era are decidedly modern.

an early childhood professional who visited a home-based care where the children spent large chunks of the day *strapped into car seats on the floor*. Those children may have technically been 'safe' compared to being left alone all day, but they were not interacting with their environment or caregiver in a way that led to any kind of learning or development. That is not "good enough" – it is the opposite of quality childcare.

The point is, instead, that quality can exist in any caregiving setting. In her recent book *Cribsheet,* economist Emily Oster plainly summarizes the research base: "[C]hildcare quality matters much more than which type of childcare you have."[71] So, while there are undoubtedly differences in what a child's day looks like when spent with his grandmother versus in a center, either path can lead to a healthy developmental trajectory. As mentioned, Section II of this book is dedicated to questions of quality and how Child Development Credits will cause quality to universally rise. But never forget this truth: quality in early childhood is defined, driven, determined at its core by the caregiver-child relationship and the environment in which that relationship exists.

Notably, research tells us high-quality early care has an especially positive impact on children from lower-income backgrounds. This is unsurprising given that, in addition to a loving family and a multitude of assets, these children have, on average, more risk factors and fewer buffering factors in their lives.

The idea that a shiny childcare center and an older neighbor's house offer the same developmental potential may feel a bit counterintuitive, but this is not mere opinion. A few years back, the National Academies of Sciences brought together an interdisciplinary team of experts to produce what would eventually be a 700-page report entitled *Transforming the Workforce for Children Birth Through Age 8: A Unifying Foundation*. They almost could have done with just producing the first page, which states plainly: "Young children thrive when they have secure, positive relationships with adults who are knowledgeable about how to support their development and learning and responsive to their individual progress."[72]

The reason for this lies in those marvelous, magical little brains.

* * *

How Brains Are Built

Human brains are primed to learn different information at different developmental stages[*]. An immense amount of foundational learning happens in the earliest years, as seen in this graph from Harvard's Center on the Developing Child[73]:

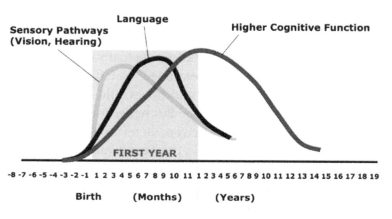

Human Brain Development
Neural Connections for Different Functions Develop Sequentially

Source: C.A. Nelson (2000)

This is part of the story behind why pre-academic gaps along socioeconomic lines begin to appear in toddlers as young as a year and a half (it's also why partially why kids are so adept at learning new languages and adults so inept). There's actually an evolutionary explanation which you may have heard before: Humans need very large heads to accommodate our sophisticated, intelligent brains. There came a point, however, where mothers couldn't pass their big-headed babies through the birth canal while also being bipedal; the pelvic physics just didn't work. Other scientists have recently added a parallel finding that keeping a fetus inside past nine months would be too taxing, energy-wise, for the mother's body.[74]

Either way, our ancestors adapted by starting to birth babies before their brains are particularly well-baked. This is why human babies are unusual in the animal kingdom in being helpless for such a long time,

---

[*] Although recent research has revealed these stages aren't as discrete as previously thought; they can and often do blend into one another, and children have wide ranges in when and how they progress.

while baby gazelles can drop out, shake off, and join the running herd. What that means is that also unusual among animals, there is a huge burst of core brain development in human babies which is highly influenced by the *external* environment, as opposed to coming hardwired. It's why the earliest months of a child's life are absolutely critical; humans have, as an ironic natural consequence of our big important brains, opened ourselves to the potential for disrupting those brains' foundational development.

Importantly, though, these first phases of brain development only last for the first eight years or so of life[*]. After that, the brain begins "pruning" back connections that are not deemed important enough to keep. That means that early childhood is a particularly crucial time because connections missed or not made strongly enough, upon which all future connections will build, simply begin to vanish (while the brain remains plastic for much longer, including another malleable spike in adolescence, the plastic does harden as time goes on). You can see this brain development arc in stark detail by looking at neural connections in a child's brain over time:[75]

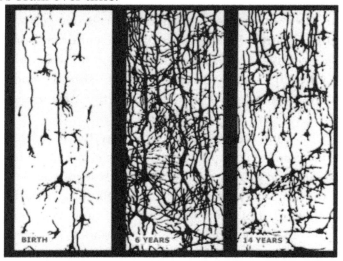

BIRTH   6 YEARS   14 YEARS

---

[*] Thanks to the history of public schools, we now consider kindergarten (age 5) as a magical cutoff point that ends early childhood; developmentally speaking, this make little sense. The shift from 'early childhood' to 'middle childhood' actually occurs somewhere in the range of ages 7 or 8, hence the title of the National Academies report. For the purposes of the Child Development Credits, I'm using age 5 as the cutoff only because that's when free public schooling becomes available.

So when we talk about early childhood, we're talking about the literal building of brains. It's worth saying yet again that how brains develop confirms the lie of distinguishing 'care' and 'education.' Secure emotional attachments, far more than the most outstanding instruction, provides the sturdiest building materials for young brains (and besides, when you have a positive caregiver-child relationship, the pair is naturally going to engage in all sorts of activities that lead to learning, from reading books to nature walks). We're wired for relationships.

You can see indisputable proof of this by looking, perhaps with gritted teeth, at severely maltreated children. Young children who have experienced major neglect or abuse show, as one research paper states, "reduced brain volumes, with alterations observed in temporal, frontal, parietal, and occipital regions, and in overall cortical gray and white matter volume."[76] Yet, there is a beacon of light in this darkness: When these maltreated children receive early intervention and are placed into loving, nurturing environments, their brain development has the potential to – and often does – normalize. Dr. Bruce Perry, a renowned child trauma expert who has worked with children from the worst imaginable circumstances, such as the young survivors of the Branch Davidian cult in Waco, Texas, puts it simply and elegantly: "Relationships are the agents of change, and the most powerful therapy is human love."[77]

This is why when families thrive, children thrive – and why, as we'll talk about in a moment, supporting families is the way through which to reach our societal goals for children. It's a research base that supports a nascent movement focusing on "early relational health" alongside children's physical and mental health.[78] Author and journalist Paul Tough writes in *How Children Succeed* about a series of studies demonstrating the long-term academic implications of secure relationships:

"Babies whose parents responded readily and fully to their cries in the first months of life were, at one year, more independent and intrepid than babies whose parents had ignored their cries. In preschool, the pattern continued – the children whose parents had responded more sensitively to their emotional needs as infants were the most self-reliant.

Warm, sensitive, parental care, [researchers] Ainsworth and Bowlby contended, created a 'secure base' from which a child could explore the world.

...In preschool, two-thirds of children in [a separate, longitudinal] Minnesota study who had been securely attached at infancy were categorized by their teachers as 'effective' in terms of their behavior, meaning they were attentive and engaged and rarely acted out in class. Among children who had been observed to be anxiously attached a few years earlier, only one in eight was placed in the effective category; the large majority of those children were classified by their teachers as having one or more behavior problems

...Finally, the researchers followed the children through high school, where they found that early parental care predicted which students would graduate even more reliably than IQ or achievement test scores. Using measures of early parenting only and ignoring the students' own characteristics and abilities, the researchers found they could have predicted with 77 percent accuracy, when the children were not yet four years old, which ones would later drop out of high school."[79]

This is simultaneously jaw-dropping and makes total sense. Child development is literally inseparable from the caregiver-child interaction.

*　　*　　*

"School Readiness" vs. "Family Support"

The diverse faces of American childcare, and the fact that no one setting is superior, are a major reason why a system of universal public childcares is a questionable solution. Early childhood defies one-size-fits-all – there can be no One Best System.

This goes to the heart of a philosophical distinction about how we spend public money on the first years of life. Whitehurst, the former U.S. Department of Education official, terms the two camps 'school readiness' and 'family support'.[80]

School readiness is the idea that the goal of government programs in early childhood is to ensure students show up in kindergarten ready to go*. In other words, it's an intervention to prevent or repair a gap. Family support is the idea that (Whitehurst quotes the Danish government here), "public authorities have an overall responsibility for providing a good social framework and for providing the best possible conditions for families with children." While I find "providing the best possible conditions for families with children" to be both a lovely and evidence-based mission statement for early childhood policy, it should not surprise you to learn that 'school readiness' is *by far* the dominant philosophy of the day in America.

The key difference is where the center of gravity is placed. In the school readiness model, the focus is on the child in a vacuum. She needs certain foundational academic knowledge and skills (knowing letters, understanding counting, etc.) and behavioral abilities (self-control, calming down) so that she can succeed in school, so we'll figure out a way to give her those. This logic naturally leads to policies like pre-K for four-year-olds: a center-based setting is the most reliable way to transfer readiness skills, and by the time a child if four, he or she has a better attention span and is fairly self-sufficient when it comes to addressing physical needs.

In the family support model, on the other hand, the family comes first. As Whitehurst puts it, that means "providing care based on the needs of parents, which means proportionate spending across the early childhood years [and not just on four-year-olds]; the availability of care that is responsive to the working hours of parents; and a requirement that initiatives taken in relation to individual children must be agreed to by the parents."

Here's the problem with our current school readiness philosophy: It doesn't make any sense. After reading the previous section, it should be clear that segmenting out four- and maybe three-year-olds ignores the dizzyingly complex and cumulative nature of child and brain development that we know starts in utero*. Recall *Neurons to*

---

* The U.S. Department of Education says so explicitly: pre-K program expenditures using Title I dollars (which are focused on low-income students) are allowed because they "improve cognitive, health, and social-emotional outcomes for eligible children ... such a program is designed to prepare eligible children with the prerequisite skills and dispositions for learning that will enable them to benefit from later school experiences."
* Before, really; the state of parents' bodies (particularly mothers) in the weeks and months – nutrition, stress levels, etc. – leading up to a pregnancy have

Neighborhoods, and a paragraph so important it needs to be repeated:

"The scientific evidence on the significant developmental impacts of early experiences, caregiving relationships, and environmental threats is incontrovertible. Virtually every aspect of early human development, from the brain's evolving circuitry to the child's capacity for empathy, is affected by the environments and experiences that are encountered in a cumulative fashion, beginning early in the prenatal period and extending throughout the early childhood years."[81]

Beginning early in the prenatal period. Not beginning at age four.

Psychologist Urie Bronfenbrenner visually captured the inextricable developmental influences of environment way back in 1979, publishing what has come to be known as his "Ecological Systems Theory."[82] You can see a version of this model in the accompanying graphic. The family support philosophy integrates nicely with what we now know is an accurate view of child development. School readiness, which zooms in tight on the child, does not.

School readiness vs. family support is not just a question of semantic difference; there's an opportunity cost. Focusing on school readiness means we pump our resources and energy into policies and programs for four-year-olds. As the National Governors Association puts it, at a time when pre-K policy is one of the hottest topics nationwide, "setting a policy agenda that specifically addresses the needs of infants, toddlers, and their families is still only an emerging concept in most corners of the country."[84]

---

been shown to have a major impact on fetal and child development. An entire field of epigenetics has arisen to investigate the way that the experience of one's lives passes down to one's children; it turns out that while DNA doesn't change over the course of your life, the genetic material it's packaged in does.

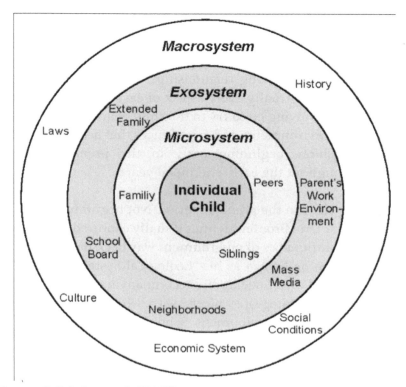

Source: Ballabeina, et. al. (2009)[83]

Interestingly, Whitehurst, an education guy through and through, comes down on the side of family support. He does so because it's a false dichotomy, one that if I've done my job as a writer, I hope you've picked up on by now: *supporting the family supports school readiness!*

Secure attachments form the basis for healthy brain development and thus, all future emotional regulation and learning. Regardless of the childcare situation, children are spending a huge number of their hours at home. Recall the research that just handing a poor family two thousand bucks does about as much as finding their kid a truly excellent teacher. The cascading effects of putting families in a place where they are not chronically stressed and in a scarcity mindset can hardly be overstated.

Stable families nearly automatically promote school readiness. While every parent adores their child, when you're not freaking out about which bill to put on which credit card, or bone-tired from working multiple jobs, it's a lot easier to get on the floor and read *The Very Hungry Caterpillar* ten times. When you can make ends meet, you're also likely to be able to secure critical elements like decent housing, which brings huge benefits for children's learning in terms of improved sleep and reduced environmental toxins. Finally, financial stability means you're much better set up to have time and capacity for selecting a high-quality childcare setting for your kid.

Now, this isn't necessarily an either-or: state pre-K programs and Head Start have helped many, many children, and providing free pre-K for 3- and 4-year-olds can stabilize both parental checking accounts and their ability to work*. But school readiness policies like public pre-K should no longer stand alone – instead, they can be folded into a family support arc. Indeed, as we'll see later, the Credit system could actually power the expansion and strengthening of public pre-K.

In the end, family support begets school readiness. School readiness efforts bereft of family support give you only marginal, not systemic, impacts. We have to reframe the approach. The best way to support families? Give them the funds they need to ensure a strong, healthy start for their children.

---

* A small number of programs also show it's feasible to bridge school readiness and family support. Early Head Start, in particular, is an impressive model that works with the families of infants and toddlers, providing both high-quality formal care along with family support in the form of things like trained home visitors, parenting classes, etc.

Chapter 3: The Broken Childcare Marketplace

What a Failed Market Looks Like

Alissa and Jacob Swartz are childcare puzzle masters. The pair live in Santa Barbara, California, with their two sons, five-year-old Eli and one-year-old Oliver. Both sets of grandparents live nearby. To hear Alissa describe their childcare routine makes one want to grab a notepad just to keep up:

Oliver is "in a home-based daycare on Monday, Thursday, and Friday mornings from 8:00am to 12:30pm. On Mondays and Fridays, Jacob picks him up on his lunch hour, brings Oliver home – where I'm working, so I pray that he naps – and then my mother-in-law comes over after she's done with her work at around 1:30pm. On Thursday, my mom picks Oliver up at 12:30pm and watches him the rest of the day. On Tuesday and Wednesday, he's watched full-time by a combination of my parents and my in-laws."

That's just Oliver.

Eli's in public school kindergarten, but kindergarten in Santa Barbara lets out at 2:30pm. After that, "he gets picked up on Mondays, Wednesdays, and Fridays by my in-laws. On Tuesdays and Thursdays, he goes to a paid after-school class – Art, Legos, that sort of thing – and is picked up at 4 pm by my mom."

Got all that?

"The scheduling headaches caused by the lack of childcare are *ridiculous*," Alissa adds. "I wish you could see my calendar. It takes a significant amount of time to schedule and keep track of everything. It's so piecemeal, and it's very frustrating."

Childcare is inherently messy and demands flexibility. Needs change by age and season and are determined by a thorny matrix of work hours, school hours, childcare provider hours, camp and after-school program schedules, availability of grandparents, and so on. This matrix is then made three-dimensional by applying family preferences, such as the desire of a parent to stay (or not stay) home, the desire for an outside caregiver from a particular religious denomination or language background, the desire for individual care vs. group care, and so forth.

These preferences can, of course, change – or be forced to change. One mother told me, "I resigned from my dream job because it just didn't make financial sense for our family. I had never intended to be a stay-at-home-parent, but the cost of childcare turned me into one." For my family, the forcing function came from an entirely different place: my wife had chosen to be home full-time with our children, but when she was pregnant with our second daughter, she was diagnosed with brain cancer. When she began treatment shortly after delivering a healthy baby, we started sending the girls to a childcare center a few days a week to build in rest breaks.

Animating – and in some cases imploding – this puzzle are questions of affordability and accessibility. Affordability we have covered at length. Accessibility is another monster. As Alissa puts it, in her area, "there is a significant lack of quality infant childcare, and while it's a little better in preschool, it's still terrible. You have to sign up right when you get pregnant, and you're still not guaranteed to be able to find a spot. Preschool registration lists fill up years in advance. Often, people will end up with huge commutes because their childcare is not convenient to their job, or compromise in safety or quality to get a spot."

Santa Barbara is not an outlier. A study by the Center for American Progress found that roughly half(!) of Americans in the 22 states analyzed live in what can be classified as a "childcare desert."[85] These are defined as census tracts with at least 50 children where there is either no formal childcare provider[*] or where there are more than three children for every one available formal slot. A different study found that roughly two-thirds of parents report having "only one" or "just a few" viable childcare options.[86]

Alissa's feelings of frustration are common. The search for childcare can put massive strain on families. Writer Liz Tracy illustrated this in an article entitled, "Trying to Find Affordable Childcare is Not the Job I Wanted"[87]:

---

[*] Remember, a formal provider is a licensed or registered center, licensed or registered family home, school-based pre-K, religiously-based program, etc.; obviously, access to nannies or family members or unlicensed care cannot be captured by this data.

"In the past month, I've spent close to 60 hours trying to secure childcare for my two-year-old son. This is not the kind of job I ever wanted. It's a high-stakes, unpaid position that often leaves me quite literally with a bellyache ... Each tour played out much the same way: My fun-loving child gleefully beelined for the toys. I would become giddy at the prospect of having a chunk of uninterrupted work time. And then reality would set in — the tours usually wrap with the bad news: it's either out of our price range, or there's yet another year-long waitlist* ... The immense emotional labor of finding help has taken a toll on me. There's a lot of pressure to find the right someone to raise your child in your absence, and there's a shocking lack of resources to help parents find quality care. I was pretty clueless about the all-around crappy options available."

Childcare deserts like these exist in urban, suburban, and rural settings (rural areas are hit particularly hard), and they cut across income levels – people with above-average income are just about as likely to live in a childcare desert as their less affluent counterparts. The scarcity is especially severe for infant care and toddler care (birth-to-three), as many providers choose not to offer it because of the very low, very expensive adult-to-child ratio requirements†. As many as *ninety-five percent* of Americans live in infant-toddler childcare deserts.[88]

In a properly functioning marketplace, the market would respond to these needs. This exceptionally high demand should lead to a huge increase in supply – Economics 101, right? Well, it's not working. Only 13,000 new childcare centers opened from 1997 to 2012, a 20 percent increase but not nearly enough to keep up with demand – just by pure population, there were nearly a million more children 0-to-5 in the U.S. after these fifteen years.[89] Worse, the number of providers began to plateau, starting in 2007 when the Great Recession hit.[90]

Nowadays, centers are actually *closing* at an increasingly rapid rate.

---

* Increasingly, centers are requiring "waitlist fees" – nonrefundable deposits that can range from $50 to several hundred dollars, just to be on a list for slots the vast majority of families will never get to use. Again, though, it's hard to really fault these small businesses that are gasping for financial breath.

† Even within the birth-to-three space, finding an open slot for infant care – generally defined as children six weeks of age to one year – is like locating the Holy Grail of childcare.

In my city of Richmond (VA), the community was rocked a few years back when two 75-year-old childcare institutions announced their closures within five months of each other.[91] Connecticut saw a *226 percent* increase in the number of closures just from 2015 (67 closures) to 2017 (219 closures).[92] Oklahoma lost more than 40 percent of its centers and home-based care providers in the past twelve years, a loss of 21,000 slots during a time period when the state's young child population increased by 17,000 kids[93] – as a result, one report noted that "an estimated 300,000" Oklahoman kids have no access to formal care.

Google essentially any state or city and "childcare closures" and the results populate with signs of the times (seriously, feel free to take a moment and try for your home state or city). You'll find examples like:

- "How Iowa's rural child-care crisis cost this town of 5,000 its only day care center"
- "Closure of Albuquerque daycare leaves parents, teachers blindsided"
- "Report: Vermont has lost childcare capacity"

The reason for what might be termed 'childcare desertification' is staring us in the face: costs of keeping the doors open are increasing, but parents are bailing out because they can't afford the fees. Most programs are operating on gossamer-thin profit margins, often less than 1 percent.[94] Fully half of the closing programs in Connecticut reported it was due to an inability to stay in the black*.

Increasingly, as we've seen, parents are turning to informal and FFN care. While we've shown there is nothing inherently worse or better about informal vs. formal care, informal types of care are inherently *shakier.* All it takes is one icy driveway, and Grandma's broken hip makes her too infirm to chase after a toddler (less gravely, even the retired neighbor taking a weeklong vacation to visit friends can be a crisis). As the Baby Boomers begin to approach their dotage, this type of care becomes an unstable proposition that more and more families have no choice but to chance.

Contrast this one more time with the common-good public education system and its five-figure annual per-pupil expenditures.

---

* It's worth noting that these closures tend to disproportionately hit providers that serve lower-income families, and there's often an interplay with states' inadequate subsidy programs.

The childcare market is broken[*]. Not a little broken. Catastrophically askew. Nothing short of a massive infusion of public money – say, robust $15,000 Child Development Credits – is going to right this sinking ship.

*　*　*

What About Universal Public Childcare Centers?

A deeper dive now about the idea of universal 'public childcare centers' as a mirror of public schools, because it may still be lingering in your mind. While it has a certain appeal, there are tremendous if not fatal problems with the idea as applied to the American context. In short, the institutionalization of childcare is misaligned with the reality that young parents need flexibility, and it fails to garner needed bipartisan support.

Providing care through a series of publicly-funded physical locations means a more-or-less uniform delivery system with more-or-less uniform hours, etc. Particularly in a nation where workers have limited protections and in most places public transportation is weak or nonexistent[†], this doesn't mesh well with non-traditional work hours (which are quickly becoming common[‡]), weekend work, part-time schedules, shifts that can change on a moment's notice, etc. A standardized solution is a dubious tool in a country so varied it's currently seeing a surge in Alissa Quart's described "Extreme Day Care" — those 24-hour providers able to absorb the children of night-shift workers.[95]

This concept also takes away a great deal of parental preference: some parents are truly uncomfortable leaving their toddler with someone who, for instance, doesn't speak their language, while others

---

[*] I'm not the only one saying this; law professor Harbach notes that "economists and social scientists have given sustained study to the functioning and failings of the childcare market, concluding that America's childcare market manifests multiple aspects of market failure."

[†] After all, public school districts solve the transportation quandary via busing. It's somehow difficult to envision a mass busing scheme for infants and toddlers.

[‡] According to a recent analysis done by Child Care Aware of America, 43 percent of all children under 18 in the United States have at least one parent who works non-standard hours (generally considered working outside of 8am-6pm and/or on weekends).

may have life circumstances that call for a nanny over a center. Moreover, there are tremendous challenges when it comes to bringing universal public centers to the rural areas of America. These areas have very high percentages of children in home-based or FFN care, and they, in general, lack the infrastructure and pool of potential early childhood teachers that would be needed to implement a widespread formal care approach[*].

Finally, to take a different angle, recall Bismarck: politics is the art of the possible, and this approach is a political non-starter for the right. It reads like a massive encroachment of government into the parental prerogative, to say nothing of the bureaucratic ballooning – the rationale behind Nixon's veto still looms large in much of red America.

Some decently-sized nations do provide universal public birth-to-five care – Chile, for instance – and many European countries offer free universal care for three- and four-year-olds. Perhaps the most instructive example, though, is just to the north in the Canadian province of Quebec.[96] Since 1997, Quebec has offered public birth-to-five daycares that are close to free; families pay between $7 and $20 a day, depending on income.

Unfortunately, Quebec shows the potential perils of such a system, as well as the fact that you can't cut corners when it comes to forming a new social good. Authorities didn't allocate adequate funds and failed to create enough public centers to meet demand. Even after allowing some private for-profit providers to utilize hefty subsidies, years-long waitlists formed and many families have been forced into the same dysfunctional unsubsidized market most Americans have to contend with[†].[97] Richer families better able to navigate the system have taken disproportionate advantage: The wealthiest quarter of Quebec's families are twice as likely as the poorest quarter to have a child in one of the public centers.

Moreover, program quality suffered as the province tried to lower

---

[*] As we'll see, most universal childcare center proposals end up using a combination of government-run public centers, community-based nonprofit providers, and private providers as a way of getting around needing to build a whole bunch of new public centers. There are decidedly not enough of any of these types of providers in most rural areas.

[†] Long waitlists are sadly a feature of almost every public childcare model around the world, including the well-regarded French "crèche" system, where in some Parisian neighborhoods the odds of getting a slot are one-in-three or worse.

the budget hit by allowing high adult-to-child ratios and cutting other quality corners, including less oversight of private providers. As a result, a 2014 study found that only 45 percent of the public centers serving toddlers and preschoolers were of "good" quality, and only 3 percent were "excellent" (almost all the rest were rated "acceptable"), with even lower ratings for private providers.[98] In other words, the standardization resulted in programs that could keep kids safe, but not necessarily provide an enriching environment with the caregiver-child interactions needed for cognitive flourishing. These are lessons we'll apply to the Child Development Credits when we talk about quality.

It's important to note that Quebec also shows some of the positives of a universal childcare system. The public centers, with their increased oversight, have at least established a floor of quality – vanishingly few are rated "poor" or below. Similarly, Quebec has improved upon the wage issue, as experienced childcare staff can make upwards of $50,000 a year (though that's still only two-thirds what equivalent K-12 teachers make).

What's more, a 2018 article in *The Atlantic* noted that "increases in the number of working mothers generate additional tax revenues and help offset the province's labor shortage caused by the province's aging population, with data suggesting that the increased productivity helps the universal-child-care program pay for itself. One study estimates that the program raised the province's annual GDP by the equivalent of about $3.9 billion.'"[99] Indeed, the positive impacts on the economy are so stirring that the head of Canada's central bank recently suggested Quebec's system should be considered nationwide because it could bring 300,000 mothers into the workforce.[100]

I am an avowed liberal, so how do I square my wariness of government-led universal childcare with my opposition to things like public school vouchers? It goes back to my earlier statement that childcare should be a common good like K-12 education, but it should not be a mirror image. K-12 is a qualitatively different enterprise than childcare. There is key content knowledge and skills that public school students need to gain to prepare them to be successful adults, and it matters at this level whether public dollars are supporting things like religious instruction versus science-based instruction. Moreover, we already have a system of 100,000 common schools with fixed costs (the electricity bill stays the same whether there are 400 students or 399), and vouchers take that per-pupil allocation out of the public system, damaging the education of those who remain[*].

In the birth-to-five realm, though, recall that the main thing children need is a healthy, warm relationship with caregivers who will interact intentionally (which requires serious skill when you have twelve little people and two adults!). The learning is largely organic – set up a stimulating environment and follow a child's curiosity, scaffolding it with language by asking questions and offering suggestions that stretch their thinking. When you read a book to a two-year-old, it's not about the content nearly so much as about the act of reading, getting them used to the idea of how print and words and stories work, to the cadence and tonality of a reader's changing voices, and so on. Whether the book they're reading happens to be about Moses doesn't really matter. And, since we *don't* currently have a system of common childcares, providing Credits doesn't cause collateral damage.

* * *

The Path to a Functional Market

In the end, it comes back to choice. Parents should be able to choose a childcare setup that works for their family and enables them to be productive members of society. That's not happening in our failed childcare market. Parents do not have the purchasing power for their demand to drive supply, and providers do not have anywhere else to turn to in order to stay solvent. The trajectory we're on is one where more and more families will either be forced to (rather than choosing to) have a parent stay home and suffer the financial consequences, or increasingly turn to cheaper, lower-quality options.

This is not fearmongering, this is the way capitalism works. Families that can't afford rent in a higher-cost area are pushed into substandard housing or geographically distant areas where their quality of life suffers from exceptionally long commutes. Families that can't afford a decent car are forced into acquiring an old, wheezing lemon that is prone

---

[*] Public charter schools are a grayer area because the per-pupil money is still being pulled out of the traditional school, but it's staying in a public system with some degree of government oversight. Reasonable people can reasonably disagree on whether that's good or bad.

to malfunctions.

Except these aren't cars, and these aren't lodgings. These are children. Substandard care for children is flat-out dangerous, both for their immediate safety and their long-term development (to say nothing of their parents' stress levels). Consider what two analysts from the Bipartisan Policy Center wrote in a *Roll Call* op-ed about the state of just our nation's physical childcare facilities, not even considering what's happening inside:

"Recent findings have been dire. A series of surveys conducted in 2013 and 2014 by the [U.S.] Department of Health and Human Services' inspector general found that 96 percent of childcare programs inspected across 10 states had at least one potentially hazardous condition, such as broken or unlocked gates, water damage, or chemicals within reach of children.

In Massachusetts, a statewide study commissioned by the Children's Investment Fund found excessive levels of carbon dioxide in childcare facilities as well as insufficient ventilation systems and furnishings containing formaldehyde. Moreover, 80 percent of programs lacked classroom sinks, which can negatively affect children's hygienic practices and infection control. Exposure to lead and other toxins has detrimental impacts on young children, yet only eight states and New York City require childcare facilities to test their drinking water for lead."[101]

It doesn't have to be this way. Give parents purchasing power, create strong guardrails, and a functional, positive market will form. Affordability leads to accessibility leads to quality. The first link in the chain is clear:

Childcare should be free for families.

Chapter 4: How Child Development Credits Would Work (And Why Stay-At-Home Parents Should Be Eligible)

Getting Concrete About Credits

Childcare should be a common good, bolstered with enough public funds to zero out the cost. Families should be supported so they can maintain stable home environments and access high-quality care as needed. The childcare marketplace is, to use the scientific term, a hot mess. The logical conclusion is to provide families with robust Child Development Credits. What exactly does that look like?

(This might be a good time to re-read "A Note on Proposals," because I'm about to get on board the proposal train.)

As a quick aside, I'm strongly in favor of a universal 'child allowance,' which many European nations and Canada have – I'll actually advocate for one in the final chapter as a needed complement to the Credits[*]. However, child allowances are generalized cash transfers, which are more amorphous by nature. The advantage of Child Development Credits is that they are focused directly on two very specific outcomes: giving families with children the ability to move up the socioeconomic ladder, and cultivating in children the foundational brain architecture they need to succeed later in life. We know what quality childcare costs, we know how much it is burdening families, and so it's a crisis we can address with precision and bipartisan support.

There are many ways to technically implement the Credit when it comes to outside care. Perhaps simplest is allowing providers to register, giving them an ID number, and then having parents fill out a form that

---

[*] I'm also personally sympathetic to the case for Universal Basic Income (UBI) – just cutting a check to everyone so there's a minimum income floor no matter your circumstances. It would serve as a *de facto* form of family support. However, I'm not yet sure a UBI meets the common-good test, and I am absolutely sure it's currently a political non-starter.

directs their $15,000 to their provider(s) of choice*. An alternative might be to issue debit cards that could only be used for care, similar to cards tied to Health Savings Accounts. The underlying concept behind the Credits is not new, so there are existing models to learn from. In particular, Minnesota's Early Learning Scholarships partially utilize just such a "money-follows-the-child" approach[†].

Once in place, Child Development Credits should have the market-reshaping impact that the GI Bill did for higher education. Remember that by giving veterans reasonable amounts of purchasing power, 270 new community colleges opened within three years, fully a fivefold increase.

Hand a $15,000 per-child Credit to each family, and you can imagine a similar flowering. Centers and home-based cares would sprout by the thousands, rushing in to meet the unfilled seven-figure demand for slots (thereby also providing an economic and jobs boost). This isn't mere speculation; after Finland passed a massive expansion of public childcare money in 1973, the number of providers quadrupled in just 15 years; by 1999, a study found there were no childcare shortages in 94 percent of Finnish municipalities.[102]

Providers would be able to specialize, offering parents choices that align with their preferences and needs. You can imagine some providers specializing in care during non-traditional hours, others offering language immersion, or being willing to take care of mildly sick kids, or able to offer transportation to and from the site, and so on. Importantly, some would be able to focus on caring for children with special needs, a group we haven't yet mentioned but one which currently has glaringly few options. In sum, the search for childcare would no longer be an act of despair and desperation, but a question of finding the best option for one's family and children.

It's likely that the overall choice of care settings would follow the patterns we see today: relatively more formal care for older children,

---

* The Credit would need to be able to be split up, as we know many families utilize multiple providers

† The component of the Minnesota program which operates like the proposed Credits has shown great promise, but it is much smaller in scope and scale. Early Learning Scholarships are targeted to 3- and 4-year-old children of families beneath 185% of the poverty line (about $46,000 for a family of four), and provide $7,500 a year to be used at an eligible provider.

relatively more informal care for infants and toddlers[*]. The Credits also integrate well with the existing subsidized care like Head Start/Early Head Start or public school pre-K, because qualifying families could just utilize their Credits for those slots as desired[†]. The Credit system would actually boost these programs by providing additional resources; for instance, the current per-child expenditure for Head Start is slightly under $10,000, and most state pre-K expenditures are significantly lower. In fact, there's no reason at all to think only private providers would flourish in this new system. Many parents will prefer a government-run program or one run by a nonprofit community-based organization; the Credits would trigger an expansion of these programs as well as a strengthening of the existing ones.

Presumably, all providers would respond to the Credits by raising their fee floor to $15,000 or the locally-adjusted equivalent. That's great. That's around what they *should* be charging. It's a fee structure that allows providers to operate in the black without being bound by the Iron Triangle[‡], and it allows them to pay their teachers a living wage (there's a strong argument to be made that the Credits should be higher for infants and toddlers, and also that formal providers should get a supplement because quality large-group care is more expensive than 1:1 or small-group care; more on these in the 'Variations' chapter). Undoubtedly some providers would charge even more for 'premium' services, and that's fine too. The point is to establish a universal threshold of availability and quality – a functional marketplace can bear providers at different price points[§].

By the way, I understand there may be some discomfort with talking about price points and profits regarding children. Know that essentially

---

[*] It's also possible entirely new types of care settings would arise. Finland, for instance, has a bevy of popular public "open childcare centers," convenient young-child-friendly locations where parents and informal providers can bring their little ones to socialize, access learning resources, and play.

[†] As we'll talk about in Section 3, it's likely that the existing childcare subsidies would be rolled up to help pay for the Credits, but the impact on the qualifying families themselves would be negligible.

[‡] Remember, as things currently stand, staying solvent = always at max enrollment, always charging fees that cover costs, and always collecting all fees on-time. Fail at any of these and you're in the red.

[§] If this did turn out to be a problem, an easy policy backstop is requiring Credit recipients to keep the fees for some percentage of their slots no higher than the local Credit amount.

no one is getting into the childcare business to make a quick buck; it's hard, demanding work, not a cash cow. There are many, many ways to make more money that involve a whole lot fewer diaper changes.

All of that said, a pure free market, unfettered, is ripe for manipulation. As we'll see in Section II, there are some frighteningly bad examples of care out there. What's needed is a free market with guardrails – a fair market. Those guardrails need to exist to fight against the negative effects of information asymmetry, which is simply the fact that providers have more knowledge about the quality of their offerings than the would-be consumer (the parents). Indeed, as Meredith Harbach notes in an article aptly titled *Childcare Market Failure*, "Multiple studies report that parents lack sufficient information about a variety of childcare characteristics – the advantages and attributes of high-quality childcare, the [indicators] of childcare quality, the location and availability of care, the relative costs of care, and information on the range of care alternatives."[103]

Happily, this is one area where states have already put in a lot of work. Nearly every state has what's known as a Quality Rating and Improvement System (QRIS) for their licensed childcare providers. This is essentially a star rating database – think Yelp – that helps parents know at a glance the quality of a program, and also helps programs engage in improving their quality (QRIS have much friendlier names like Parent Aware, Quality Start, Colorado Shines, etc.). Quality measures range from basic health and safety to elements like having a teaching force with a certain level of credentials/degrees, implementing ongoing training, adopting a vetted curricula, reaching certain benchmarks on classroom observations by independent raters, and so on. Participation in the QRIS is voluntary in some states, but in several like Arkansas and Louisiana, it's mandatory if a program wants to be eligible to receive public subsidy dollars. Similarly, Minnesota's Early Learning Scholarships mentioned earlier can only go to programs that have enrolled in the state's QRIS.[104]

And here is the other side of the voucher coin: In order to ensure a fair market, any Credit-eligible provider will need to get accredited. This is a reasonable expectation for any organization that's about to get a huge influx of taxpayer funds, whether in childcare or another field. For instance, federal financial aid for college, such as Pell Grants, can only be used at accredited institutions. Accreditation means that we can ensure quality in addition to access, and we can provide parents with information to make them savvy consumers.

Accreditation would look different for different forms of care. For formal providers, accreditation would mean enrolling in their state's QRIS. Several states also have a modified QRIS designed for informal home-based providers[*]. A light-touch accreditation will need to be developed for individual providers like nannies, perhaps requiring a minimum number of (paid) training hours per year. Relatives providing FFN care who want to receive the Credit would similarly need to receive an individual accreditation, although if they are providing care for free and wish to continue doing so, they're welcome to decline accreditation. That's one of the selling points here: no one's forcing anyone to do anything.

The goal of accreditation isn't to micromanage but to make sure that providers have the supports they need to provide at least a floor of quality. Recall the National Academies' conclusion: "Young children thrive when they have secure, positive relationships with adults who are knowledgeable about how to support their development and learning and responsive to their individual progress." As I can attest, forming those positive relationships with young children can be difficult at times; even moreso knowing how to follow their lead while stretching their thinking. In the next section, we'll look at examples of what these types of trainings can look like, based on examples that already exist.

One part of the sector remains a question mark we can't put off tackling any longer, though: What happens for stay-at-home parents?

*   *   *

Whither Stay-At-Home Parents?

This is perhaps the most contentious part of the proposal because it reaches directly into an area Harbach describes as quadruply private ("a private matter, involving private prerogatives, provided in the private

---

[*] Accreditation for the purposes of the Credits would need to be distinct from current licensure standards: for instance, some home-based providers are ineligible for licensure because they lack an adequately-sized backyard; that sort of thing shouldn't be a barrier to receiving the Credits. This is about broad sunlight, not exclusion.

home, and a matter of private responsibility"); put another way, parent-provided care has long been seen as heavily removed from public intervention.

The beauty of a Child Development Credit system is that it acknowledges stay-at-home parents are doing the socially beneficial work of preparing their children to be successful and productive adults *without taking over the parenting*.

Preserving parents' choice to stay home and raise their children – just as we want to preserve their choice to work outside the home – is key. Even the way we refer to such individuals as 'stay-at-home parents' feels like a vaguely negative euphemism, as if set against the 'real' work that 'leaving-the-home' parents do. Yet there is little more meaningful, difficult, or societally critical work than cultivating the next generation. This issue rears its head with particular intensity for women, who inarguably bear the brunt of our competing expectations. After all, we increasingly expect (or implicitly require) mothers to work in order to balance the household budget, yet recall the 2013 survey which found half of Americans think young kids are better off when cared for by their mother. Our refusal to compensate stay-at-home mothers is the clasp on this double-bind. Author Vanessa Olorenshaw puts it this way:

"Whereas once our place was mandated to be at home, it is now firmly in the workplace. There is no flexibility. No recognition of the diversity in mothers' wishes, skills, inclinations or needs, or the validity of mothers taking a short or longer period of time out of continuous workplace participation in order to do the important work of care ... We talk about the feminization of poverty[*] without stopping to acknowledge that a significant reason women face poverty is because we, still, refuse to put money in their hands to reflect the valuable work they do. The unwaged work of children and home."[105]

Olorenshaw is spot-on when she refers to a diversity of mothers' wishes. As a male, I'm very cautious when it comes to speaking about women's preferences, so it's helpful to look at hard data – and all the data agrees there is a wide variety of preferences. For instance, in a 2012 Pew survey that asked married mothers what their "ideal" work situation

---

[*] A disproportionate percentage of individuals below the poverty line are female.

would be, 47 percent said working outside the home part-time, 32 percent said working outside the home full-time, and 20 percent said not working outside the home at all (other surveys have found that these preferences, perhaps unsurprisingly, are dynamic – they change based on the age of the children and other factors*).[106]

It's time to start putting money in stay-at-home parents' hard-working hands.

For a stay-at-home parent to get the Credit, they should just certify to the government using their social security number that they're the one primarily taking care of their young child, and the $15,000 comes to them in monthly installments. There will presumably need be a smaller payment for additional children (e.g. $15k for the first child, $5k for the second, etc.), which is a model used by most European nations that offer stipends for stay-at-home parents. Those details, while important, are secondary to the importance of folding these parents into the Credit system.

Since it's clear many caregiving parents prefer or need to work part-time, the Credit should be pro-rateable (if you're caregiving during work hours for 20 hours a week, you get $7,500; same if you caregive full-time for six months before returning to the workforce, etc.). Parents can and should be offered a whole suite of voluntary resources – free children's books, online parenting modules, connections to local services, etc. – but there can be no hoops to jump through. Parents are always accredited to take care of their own children†.

As noted above, this isn't a new idea. Many European nations that offer a version of free public childcare have an opt-out for stay-at-home parents that comes with a cash stipend. Going back to Finland for a moment, stay-at-home parents there can get the equivalent of $4,200 a year from the time a child is born until he or she turns three years old.[107] Compensating a parent for acting as a caregiver isn't even a new idea in America, if you look beyond children: in many states, family members,

---

* There are also significant differences in answers between married and unmarried mothers.
† It may be reasonable to require that for those doing full-time parental care during their child's fourth year of life, and who plan to use the local public school, that child attend a (free) summer Kindergarten transition session. That session would allow the child to learn the ins and outs of 'doing' school so that he or she isn't at a disadvantage come the first day. These types of transition programs are already offered in many states and localities.

including parents, can be paid through Medicaid or other programs to act as a home health care provider for a disabled (or elderly) relative.[108]

Matt Bruenig of the People's Policy Project suggests that for the U.S., a childcare opt-out stipend should be equal to the median salary of a childcare worker, but proportionally reduced to the number of children the parent is caring for*. You can read the preceding footnote for more detail, or if you care less about the math, just know that using 2018 wages Bruenig calculates the parental stipend as $5,730 per child. That formula is certainly an option for the U.S., though I might argue that for a common good, no one type of care should get below the base Credit amount. Conveniently though, if the Credits allowed childcare workers to start making the median salary of elementary school teachers, the cash opt-out using Bruenig's formula would come to about $14,000, so perhaps it's a distinction without much difference.

One tremendous benefit of paying stay-at-home parents is that it serves as a form of paid parental leave. The U.S. is one of the worst in the world at providing paid leave to mothers and fathers, despite what we know about the essential bonding and brain building that happens during the earliest weeks of life. A truly sickening number of women — nearly a quarter of employed mothers of newborns! — are back at work *two weeks* after giving birth, which from a purely physical standpoint should make us all feel ashamed.[109] Being able to temporarily use the Credit, when combined with the job-protecting federal Family and Medical Leave Act, gives parents at least a modest amount of *de facto* paid leave[†].

Three objections regarding the Credits have likely jumped into

---

* Bruenig: "So, for instance, the median childcare worker has an annual salary of $22,290. The recommended child-to-adult ratio for these workers is around four to one depending on the age of the child. Dividing $22,290 by four gives $5,730 per year, which is $110 per week. Thus, under prevailing child-to-adult ratios and prevailing childcare worker wages, the weekly home childcare benefit would be $110 per child. If the ratios or prevailing wages change, e.g. because the new public childcare system sets higher wages, then the home childcare allowance would change with it." The median elementary teacher salary in 2017 was $57,160, which gets you a cash opt-out of $14,290 per year.

† While some businesses may not love the idea of paid parental leave policies, they've never been pitched parental leave in combination with free childcare once the worker returns, which makes up for those weeks of leave by minimizing lost productivity, days off, and transience due to childcare problems.

readers' throats by now: what about fraud, won't it make parents stop working, and why are we suddenly paying parents to take care of the kid *they* chose to have?

First, in general, fraud rates in all sorts of different cash transfer programs – social security, SNAP (food stamps), etc. – are *extremely* low, hovering around 1 percent.[110] Flipped, that means that 99 percent of the funds are being used as intended. There's no reason to think it would be any different for Child Development Credits.

Second, $15,000 is deep poverty wages – it's roughly equal to a full-time, full-year's work at the federal minimum wage of $7.25 an hour. It's a huge boost for a family that already has someone working full-time where the caregiving partner would otherwise make zero dollars. But if the family budget requires a second earner bringing in substantial income, then $15,000 a year isn't going to cut it (and hey, if the opportunity to care for one's own child forces McDonalds to raise its wages to be more competitive, so be it).

That said, taking the perspective of poor parents, it's not hard to construct a hypothetical where there's an incentive to pull down the cash to meet basic survival needs (food, shelter) and find a cheap 'gray market' option for childcare. Evidence from other nations with cash opt-outs suggests that this can happen at times, although the frequency is highly uncertain.[111] This potential problem highlights the critical need for the Credits to be coupled with additional boosts for poor families. Boosts could look like an unrestricted child allowance, expansion of the Earned Income Tax Credit, or other measures that ensure lower-income parents aren't forced to choose between feeding their children and utilizing high-quality care[*].

Third, we're paying parents to care for their own children because, guess what, they're *providing for the common good.* To put a fine point on it, the child of a stay-at-home parent is tomorrow's kindergartener, and again, the evidence of what the earliest years can do for brain development and later academic and life success is overwhelming[†].

---

[*] Though, to be honest, this isn't a disastrous policy outcome: We know that providing poor families with cash transfers alone does wonders for their stability and for the outcomes of both parents and children.

[†] The reason we don't pay homeschooling K-12 parents is because they're electing to remove themselves from an existing universal public system. This is also a place where the distinct developmental periods of early childhood vs. middle childhood and adolescence come into play.

Recall Katharine Stevens' truism that "the commonly made distinction between 'care' and 'education' in early childhood is a false one." The point can hardly be made enough times that caring for young children is demanding, skillful work; the fact that the work may be gilded with a parent's love doesn't devalue the fact that it's work*. In America, work is supposed to be the ideal, and work is supposed to be compensated.

And yes, these parents chose to have children, but guess what? We need children. In fact, we need a lot more than we currently have. Just during the writing of this book, an article in the *Washington Post* declared: "As U.S. Fertility Rates Collapse, Finger-Pointing and Blame Follow."[†112] The article reported on new data from the Centers for Disease Control showing fertility rates (the number of births women will theoretically have in their lifetime) plummeting in the past decade by double-digit percentages across all racial and income categories. The U.S. fertility rate is now at 1.76, significantly below the 'replacement rate' of 2.1 where births equal deaths.

Too few children and society faces a full-blown crisis like the one Japan, and several other nations are currently staring down‡. Lyman Stone, a population economist, paints the picture: "If we fail [to raise the fertility rate], putting it plainly, the future will include insolvency of our social aid for the elderly and the poor, a permanent decline in economic dynamism, huge swaths of the country locked in intergenerational economic depression and an ever-increasing burden on women in particular, as family life becomes less compatible with a career."[113] We'll

---

* This fact caused a flare-up in the 1970s, when a strike of 25,000 Icelandic women over gender inequality led to major reforms in that country. The U.S. "Wages for Housework" movement was less successful but still laid important groundwork for future conversations around expectations of women.
† There's also been an increase in headlines like this one from public radio station WAMU in April 2019: "Why Is Childcare So Expensive? Costs Leave Washington [D.C.]-Area Millennials Hesitant To Have Kids." To be fair, the drop in fertility isn't entirely due to childcare issues; women are on average having their first babies later in life (and there's been a significant and welcome decline in teen pregnancy), which in general reduces the total number of children they will have.
‡ There are a complex web of factors that go into Japan's issues with low birth rates which I don't pretend to be able to speak to, but I'll point out correlatively that the nation faces a major undersupply of public childcare slots, parents are struggling to afford private slots, and there's recently been a big debate over whether the government should be providing zero-cost care options. Sound familiar?

cover this topic at greater length later in the book, including showing how stabilizing fertility rates and stabilizing families more broadly, can be one key step towards addressing global warming.

So the question isn't so much why should we pay stay-at-home parents – it's why haven't we been valuing stay-at-home parents enough to compensate them all this time?

*   *   *

Indeed, it is emphatically *not* just the two-earner set that is hit hard by the childcare crisis. Many families where a parent has chosen to stay home, thus nearly zeroing out external childcare costs, are fighting to survive in the modern economy.

Ruth and Jared Watt live in a small rural town of less than 5,000 people. Both are college graduates, and Jared works as an assistant professor at a nearby university. Devout Catholics, the Watts are the grateful (if tired) parents of six children aged 10 and younger, including three younger than 5. Ruth stays home full-time with the kids, homeschooling the older ones.

Ruth shares that the primary reasons for her staying home are twofold: First, religious conviction animating a desire to lean into the work and joy of raising a large family every step of the way; and second, a realization that if she worked outside the home, essentially all of the earnings would be swallowed up by childcare fees.

Again, this is a perfectly valid choice, just as valid as the choices of the other couples we've met. Like those other couples, the Watts completed the "Millennial Success Sequence" – and, what's more, they're raising a big family in an era when, as we've just seen, the American birth rate is plummeting. Yet the sacrifices that go along with this choice are monumental. The sacrifices are also critical to understand, given that nearly one in three families currently has a stay-at-home parent. Ruth is frank about the impacts: "A reduced income has affected every decision we make."

She explains further: "We do not buy new clothes, and while we are fortunate enough to receive gifts and hand-me-downs to supply our needs, we also wear lots of clothes with stains, holes, and rips. Yes, our kids mostly don't care about wearing nice clothes, but it's still embarrassing for them to wear dress shoes with black electrical tape on them. The only vehicle we currently have is not large enough to safely transport all the members of our family, and we have had to decline invitations to many social gatherings because we can't afford the gas to get there. I regularly refuse medical testing that doctors recommend, such as radiology and lab work during pregnancy, because we cannot afford a babysitter for the appointments."

Simply put, Ruth says, "I just need more help."

Paying stay-at-home parents via the Credits would both inject financial stability into the lives of one-earner families and show them the respect they deserve. While some may judge the choices of the struggling dual-earner families (why don't they move somewhere cheaper where one parent can stay home?), the fact that dual-earner households are now the norm largely insulates them from criticism. Struggling single-earner families, however – particularly those with high numbers of children – get side-eyed in much of America because it feels like they're leaving one potential earner benched. The double-bind, redux.

Ruth is painfully aware of the silent judgment. "I am perfectly convinced now, ten years into it, that my kids are worth this struggle," she says, "but I am not sure that many other people see it that way. I'm not sure they see the value in my kids' existence, and I fear that they think that any of my kids past number three was just a foolish compounding of our problems, that I deserve whatever difficulty I face as a result."

This goes to the fact that stay-at-home parents often experience a type of social isolation on top of their financial straits, compounding the all-too-common feelings of despair. In a 2012 Gallup poll, stay-at-home mothers reported significantly higher levels of anxiety, sadness, and depression than employed mothers (stay-at-home fathers weren't surveyed).[114] Only 55 percent said they were "thriving," compared to 63 percent of employed mothers. Unsurprisingly, low-income stay-at-home moms struggled even more, with only 46 percent saying they were thriving.

Let's be crystal clear: This in no way, shape, or form suggests there's something "better" about being an employed mother vs. a stay-at-home mother (or vice versa). What the data reflects is the fact that stay-at-home parents get precious little support of any kind in contemporary America. Ruth comments that her saving grace has been the local homeschooling community. "These other stay-at-home parents are the ones who help me figure out how to live a frugal life and love my kids and not go crazy. I need that almost as much as I need money." Thinking back to how few communal hands have been offered outside of that group, she adds poignantly, "My problem is partly a money problem, but it's also partly a people problem."

Of course, there are linkages between the money problem and the people problem*. When families have more means (and therefore don't have to worry about gas money, etc.), they're more able to engage in communal activities, in turn bolstering relationships that lead to offers of help and less isolation. From the other direction, if the community puts our money where our mouths are regarding the importance of families, then compensating stay-at-home parents should make their hard work both visible and worthy of lifting up.

Ruth shares a story of a particularly traumatic trip to the grocery store shortly after her third child was born. The kids' behavior in the store had started to go awry, as so many of us parents have experienced, but Ruth had no support. She recalls, "I had a five-year-old pushing a stroller with a three-week-old in it because he was the only help I had. He tipped the stroller over in the produce section, and then all three of us were crying right next to the tomatoes. I pushed the cart with two kids and all the groceries in it and pulled the stroller through the rest of the store. I was still bleeding from birth. I was terrified to leave the house, couldn't afford a babysitter, and felt as though I couldn't ask anyone to do it unless I could pay. My husband was desperately trying to finish his dissertation so he could get a job, and we'd finally have money for a babysitter."

This is not what a healthy, family-centered society looks like. This is not what a nation that embraces the family support goal of creating the "best possible conditions for families with children" looks like.

We're facing a future where fewer and fewer parents even get the choice of whether to stay home and raise their children full-time. From a standpoint of both healthy child development and family stability, we're already in a day where many stay-at-home parents are needlessly stressed and depressed. Compensating stay-at-home parents should be a non-negotiable part of any universal childcare system.

---

* It's worth mentioning that the "people problem" is also partially a symptom of a society-wide trend towards disconnection, one that impacts dual-earner families as well. By nearly any measure, we have weaker communal and relational bonds today than in the past. For stay-at-home parents, the problem is compounded by the lack of even having an external workplace to potentially provide connection.

* * *

Youth Development Credits, Too

One last point for this chapter, amidst all this talk of children: Child Development Credits need a sibling.

Your child hit their fifth birthday, and the celebration is a little extra exuberant because guess what – they can go to free public school in the fall! All of your financial woes of the past five years are in the past…

…and then you look more closely at the school calendar.

Most elementary schools let out around 3pm. Most workplaces do not.

Most school systems let out for three months in the summer. Most workplaces do not.

And you know what that means: more childcare costs!

The costs associated with after-school and summer care are obviously nowhere near the backbreaking amounts of the birth-to-five years. School takes up around seven hours of the day, the summer is finite, and kids are of an age where they can be with big groups, and so costs go down.

That said, after-school and summer care still presents a major financial challenge for many families. According to the nonprofit Afterschool Alliance, average costs for an afterschool program in 2014 were $113 a week.[115] The standard school year has 26 weeks in it, so that's about $3,000. Summer care-related costs are often estimated to average around $1,000.[116] While it may be possible in some places to find cheaper options (city-run camps, the local YMCA), costs add up quickly especially when you have multiple school-aged kids.

These high costs again lead to undesirable choices: because we're no longer talking about helpless toddlers, many families turn to "self-care" – not meditation and massages, but having children just take care of themselves for a few hours. Nationally, over a third of high schoolers, about one-in-five middle schoolers, and 3 percent of elementary schoolers are on their own after the bell rings (and researchers think these numbers are probably on the low end, as many parents don't want to admit their kids are home alone). It's also common to ask the twelve-year-old to be in charge of the six-year-old.

Self-care isn't some inherently awful thing. It may actually be positive for a high school junior to manage himself for an hour or two until his dad returns. It's different, however, when talking about a 7th grader home alone all late afternoon and evening because her mom is working nights at the hospital. A hefty body of research finds that on the whole, high-quality after-school and summer programs have a raft of positive benefits for the academic and social performance of youth, particularly youth from historically disenfranchised populations — including helping kids avoid the dreaded "summer slide."[117]

All of the arguments for why childcare should be free to families from birth-to-five apply to childcare outside of the K-12 school day/year. It's just an extension of the common good with the same double benefits for working families and youth outcomes. Unlike early childhood, though, there is a reasonably healthy after-school and summer care sector, and, as mentioned, the costs are lower. Providing families a $1,000 annual Youth Development Credit for each child between the ages of 5 and 18 ensures that at least some after-school and summer care is available to everyone[*].

While ideally childcare would be free for all ages, all hours, and all months, there are 54 million American children ages 5-18, making for an eye-popping multiplier. So, it's back to the well of compromise. Making after-school and summer care universally accessible and much more affordable is the 'next best'.

*   *   *

In the end, with Credits in hand, we would have a fundamentally different childcare landscape than we have today. The Swartzes and those like them wouldn't have to juggle so many balls or rely so heavily on the grandparents (unless they wanted to), instead able to access options that worked for their schedules. The Watts and other single-earner families would be able to focus on enjoying their boisterous brood instead of worrying about how to pay for school supplies. Throughout America, both families and children would increase their level of thriving. And in childcare settings themselves, quality would improve across the board as teacher salaries rise, quality systems and resources become widely adopted, and a little good old-fashioned American competition drives the sector forward.

Let's take a look.

---

[*] The implementation (programs registering, etc.) could mirror that of the proposed Child Development Credit

SECTION II: A CHANGED SYSTEM

Chapter 5: Quality in Formal Care

High- vs. Low-Quality Formal Care

My children, mostly in a stroke of luck, attend a high-quality childcare program[*]. I know this qualitatively because I've worked in the early childhood education sector and seen many different programs, and I know this quantitatively because their center is one of only a handful in Virginia to be rated Level 5, the highest level, on the state's quality rating and improvement system. In this chapter, we're going to look at the formal care landscape and what Child Development Credits could mean for transforming it.

What does high-quality care look like? We know by now that at the broadest level, it looks like adults interacting with children in ways that intentionally cultivate their development, and doing so in environments set up to do the same.

At my children's center, the teachers follow the kids' lead and then stretch their thinking. Erika Christakis says that the key difference between high- and low-quality formal care programs is this focus on "building relationships ... and paying a lot of attention to children's thinking processes and, by extension, their communication."[118] For instance, when some of Alma's classmates became interested in insects they found on the playground, this led to a widespread exploration of bugs. Through activities tied to this naturally occurring intrigue, the children gained more than just important scientific knowledge about

---

[*] I mean that honestly: I happened to be working for an early childhood nonprofit when my wife was diagnosed with cancer, and one of my colleagues knew of a high-quality center minutes from our house which by chance at that moment had a few part-time slots open.

insects and ecosystems. They were practicing foundational skills like comparing and contrasting different critters, counting legs, making representative drawings, and understanding nonfiction books.

The beauty of early childhood education done well is that there is no distinction between play and learning. The kids didn't know they were building numeracy and literacy skills, they were just having a grand ol' time crowding around to examine fascinating bugs; one of their teachers joked to me that every insect in Richmond had visited their classroom by the time they were done.

For infants, this high-quality interaction is more subtle but equally as important. It's the teacher who is paying attention to what the baby is pointing at and naming it as a dog, responding to the child's babbles as they learn the rudiments of language ("serve and return"), reading book after book to them – all while simultaneously attending to their physical needs and development.

What does lower-quality care look like? It doesn't look like one red flag.

Lower-quality care can look like less stimulating environments, where there may be a few worn-out books or raggedy toys. That environment may barely maintain a minimum standard of health and safety, and the food on offer may consist largely of less nutritious options like potato chips and sugary juices. Child-to-teacher ratios may be high, and the teachers may have precious little training of any kind, much less formal education in child development. It also looks like caregivers unable to form warm relationships or keep basic order; no one expects a toddler classroom to necessarily be calm (ha!), but the lack of general behavior management can turn classrooms into little more than holding pens. At rock bottom, it can look like one adult watching 59(!!) children ages one to four in massive violation of regulations, as was witnessed in 2016 at one Mississippi center.[119]

Yet, heartbreakingly, the quality of care often has to take a backseat to bank accounts. Lindsey and Jeff Copeland (not their real names) live in Denver, CO; like so many middle-class families we've met, they're both employed – she's a nonprofit professional, he's a lawyer. Despite this, when their second child came along, Lindsey explains that "we had to make the decision to pull our toddler out of his childcare program because we couldn't afford to have two kids in high-quality childcare; the fees were just too high."

After evaluating their options, the Copelands decided that a nanny was the best route for their newly expanded family[*]. Yet Lindsey and Jeff had to wrestle with the fact that "there's a really tough balance in determining the level of quality with what you can afford." Lindsey recalls interviewing a reference for a particularly inexpensive nanny the Copelands were considering. The reference was clear the only important thing was that her son was safe, and the cheap nanny could at least assure that – the reference "knew that her child wouldn't be getting the kind of quality care that she wanted, but she just couldn't afford it." The Copelands eventually found a nanny they are satisfied with, but, achingly, Lindsey adds that "we know that our current nanny isn't giving our toddler the level of education that he was receiving at his childcare center." Remember, quality that leads to optimal child development can exist in any setting, but quality does exist.

These tradeoffs are very real, and they stare many, many families in the face – mine included. My children attend their center two days a week and are home with their mother the rest of the time; if we wanted them to go every day, we couldn't afford it without seriously reworking our lives. We're at least fortunate enough to have an exceptionally high-quality option for their part-time care. In one survey, fully four in ten families said that they wouldn't characterize the care their children was receiving as "excellent" – and parents are notoriously easy graders when it comes to self-reporting on the choices they make for their kids[†].

*　　*　　*

The gold-standard rating system for formal childcare providers is known as CLASS (unimaginatively, this stands for the CLassroom Assessment Scoring System).[120] CLASS breaks down quality into different buckets depending on age level: for instance, for 3- and 4-year-olds, the buckets are Classroom Organization, Emotional Support, and Instructional

---

[*] Unlike a childcare center, where there is often no sibling discount and families just end up paying full cost twice, a nanny can be more cost-effective in these situations; nannies are an expensive option for a solo child, but rates usually only go up a few dollars an hour when adding in a second kid (hence the rising popularity of 'nanny shares,' where unrelated couples pool their children and split the costs).

[†] The "Lake Woebegone" effect shows up in that most parents agree that the nation's public schools are only so-so, but almost all say their kid's school is doing great! It's understandably very hard to admit you'd send your child to anything but the best.

Support[*]. Classroom Organization refers to behavior management and how the day is structured; Emotional Support refers to the presence of a warm, welcoming climate; and Instructional Support refers to the intentional cultivation of pre-academic knowledge and skills (like the bug unit)[†]. While this can sound stilted or technical, it's exactly what most parents intuitively provide their children – the trick here is creating that environment for group care settings.

One thing is clear: you can't have high-quality childcare without talented caregivers and teachers, any more than you can have high-quality medical care without a force of talented doctors and nurses. It's also clear we're never going to have a sustainable, high-quality early childhood workforce if we're paying poverty wages.

In group care settings, there's way less one-on-one time where you can just take the child to a park and let his or her whims dictate the day's wonders. The environments need to be more curated, and the teachers need to know how to, by observation, quickly judge what each child needs to push their thinking. There's also the obvious need to be able to set up classroom routines and respond to the emotional needs (and physical needs, and behavioral needs...) of a host of tiny people with very immature brains and very low impulse control. This is skillful, demanding work that calls for different knowledge and abilities than the skillful, demanding work of caring for a single child. This is also why licensed formal care settings tend to use a curriculum, follow "standards,"[‡] and so on. As such, formal care calls for formal training.

Yet, as we've seen, early childhood teachers are paid a pittance. Unlike almost all other employment fields, there is generally no financial incentive whatsoever for a private center teacher to get an additional degree unless they plan on changing jobs. The centers literally can't afford to give them a wage boost. This would be like a

---

[*] For infants, there's only one bucket: Responsive Caregiving.

[†] On the whole, providers tend to score higher on Classroom Organization and Emotional Support than Instructional Support.

[‡] These aren't standards in the same way that K-12 education has standardized tests (early childhood assessments are almost entirely observational or based on the teacher asking children to complete a given task, like writing their first name next to a self-portrait). Childcare standards are more a set of foundational skills for teachers to incorporate into play-based activities. For instance, Virginia's standards for 4-year-olds include things like being able to "describe how shapes are similar and different" and "distinguish print from pictures" in books.

journeyman electrician getting her master's degree in electrical engineering and then going back to the same job, making no additional money; it violates every economic rule we've been told to follow as workers.

Teachers that do get an additional degree usually do so because it makes them eligible for relatively higher-paying roles like in Head Start or state-sponsored pre-K (or, many simply make the logical choice of fleeing to teach Kindergarten or 1st grade and make tens of thousands dollars more with solid health insurance)[*]. But recall that the vast, *vast* majority of children are being served in private centers, home-based care, or with family, friends & neighbors. For all the attention they receive, Head Start, Early Head Start, and state pre-K merely make up what a former colleague called a "cottage industry" within early childhood[†]. That means that the bulk of childcare providers are left with a constant churn of less-trained teachers.

And, even if a teacher wanted to gain credentials simply for the sake of improving her craft, she's often in no position to do so. Recall that around half of early childhood teachers are making such little income that they qualify for public assistance. Many have children of their own for whom they struggle to find childcare. They're working full-time, and often working a second job or taking on babysitting shifts to boost their meager pay (at least half the teachers at my daughters' center babysit, and it's uncomfortable to know how overqualified they are). This is not the ideal setup for continuing education. While several states have scholarships available for early childhood teachers and are attempting innovative technology-based ways to make courses more accessible, our workforce development efforts continue to be a well-intentioned band-aid.

*　　*　　*

---

[*] Indeed, every time a state or city implements an expanded public pre-K system for four-year-olds, one unintended consequence is an exodus of teachers from private and nonprofit centers to the new public programs thanks to the significantly better wages. Good for the teachers, good for the pre-Ks, but it badly exacerbates the labor shortage and high rate of closures for programs that serve infants and toddlers.

[†] It's also a sad fact that even within that cottage industry, a bachelor's degree in early childhood education offers literally the lowest lifetime earning potential of any collegiate major.

The Quality-Money Connection

Quality costs money. There's no other way around it. In group care settings, it costs money to have better-trained and better-compensated teachers, and it costs money to maintain a rich environment with plenty of books, nutritious food, etc. Yet in our current broken market, I once heard a story of a local center in Richmond that was losing talented teachers *to Walmart* – Walmart offered equivalent pay and better benefits!

This cost is not theoretical. A few years back, a group of advocates in Wisconsin, utilizing a research-based cost modeling tool, decided to see how much more it would cost to run a high-quality (5-star) center versus a lower-quality (2-star) center.[121] The average per-child cost for the 2-star center came out to $9,000 a year – in other words, if the center was at full enrollment all year and paid its teachers poorly, it could charge parents $9,000 a year and just about break even.

The 5-star center? By assuming that the teachers all have associate degrees in early childhood and are making the average associate degree-holder salary for Wisconsin, the per-child average jumps to $12,745 a year. Unless the center started magically coming up with about $3,000 a kid[*] – and since that would have to come from parent fees, good luck! – it would find itself running an annual deficit of nearly $150,000, well on its way to joining the overfull graveyard of closed providers. Keep in mind that this actually a conservative estimate: take the teachers up to having bachelor's degrees and equivalent pay to kindergarten teachers, and the needed per-child average starts approaching $20,000.[122]

Where is that money going? A Center for American Progress report breaks down the average dollar distribution, which shows – as it should be – that staffing costs are the biggest cost drivers.[123] Childcare is a human endeavor, and you simply cannot skimp on the human capital without hurting quality.

---

[*] The math isn't exact because there are some cost efficiencies that can be realized; the cost model is a dynamic equation.

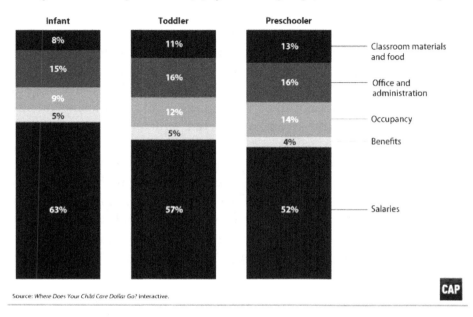

FIGURE 2

Personnel costs are the largest expense for child care programs

Distribution of child care program expenses for an infant, toddler, and preschooler in a child care center meeting basic state licensing standards and paying current average wages, based on United States averages

Infant	Toddler	Preschooler	
8%	11%	13%	Classroom materials and food
15%	16%	16%	Office and administration
9%	12%	14%	Occupancy
5%	5%	4%	Benefits
63%	57%	52%	Salaries

Source: *Where Does Your Child Care Dollar Go?* interactive.

CAP

Yet in our current money-starved system, the center's options are to run a lower-quality program and barely scrape by, or run a higher-quality program and fail. This is the choice wrought by the lack of publicly-financed childcare. Which path do you want your child's program to take?

*   *   *

Perverse Incentives Are Harming Our Kids

There is, unfortunately, a third path. It leads you to a marshland of low-quality formal providers. These providers don't even try to interact with their state's star-rating system or accept public subsidy dollars, and by doing so, they can remain weakly regulated. Christakis notes that "in some parts of the country ... the care of dead people in funeral homes is more tightly regulated than the oversight of living children in early education and care settings." This setup can lead to major abuses. A shocking illustration came a few years back when the Center for

Investigative Reporting published an expose on an Alabama provider named Deborah Stokes.[124] The reports reads in part:

"She ran a church daycare from a decrepit warehouse that one worker called a 'house out of a horror movie.' She opened another childcare center next to a porn store.

Each of her daycares has been dogged by complaints of abuse and neglect. Workers said she hit children with flyswatters, locked them in closets or rapped them with rulers. She's failed to pay so many employees that one reportedly slapped her in the face and another threatened to hurl a pickle jar at her, according to police reports.

She has been arrested multiple times, for crimes ranging from theft to child endangerment.

In total, Deborah Stokes has operated at least a dozen Christian daycares across southern Alabama. Every time she is chased out of town by furious parents, workers or landlords, she reopens in the next town over. In the process, she has collected at least $86,000 in taxpayer funding to run her daycares with almost no oversight.

She doesn't need a license. She doesn't need a curriculum or qualified workers. All she needs is a building with a roof, desperate parents, and a piece of paper saying she runs a church*."

While that story might seem like a war cry for more oversight, just because a center is technically licensed and regulated is no guarantee of anything approaching reasonable quality. A report on Texas childcares that followed the tragic 2013 death of a Houston child noted that "Like most states, Texas inspects childcare centers at least once a year, but only has the manpower to visit home daycares every two. Even egregious violations don't always lead to shutdowns. Sometimes, that's because parents, lacking alternatives, fight to keep notorious places open ... On other occasions, the process of closing a daycare can be torturous. [Former state official Sue] Lahmeyer recalled one place that racked up repeated violations over two years before a judge would shut it down. 'I can tell you there's a fair number [of cases] that we lost because the judge decided, *No child's died yet*, so they stay open.'"[125]

This, of course, says nothing about illegally operating childcare providers who are completely off the grid. These are nearly impossible

---

* In many states, there are significant regulatory exemptions for religiously-based providers (of which the vast majority are, of course, perfectly fine).

to detect absent someone making a report to the state.[126] While there's no hard data on the number of illegal providers, a moderately-sized state like Washington State gets about 250 complaints each year and eventually takes action against around 100 illegal providers; it's safe to assume that's a tiny fraction of the true number who are operating.

Put another way, the broken childcare market is actively harming children – and this is within formal care, hypothetically the type of care with the most sunlight! Think about the statements in the paragraphs above: Deborah Stokes needed desperate parents; Texas parents fight the shutdown of known abysmal-quality providers because they don't have any other options. Without enough money in the system, parents can't leverage the power of choice to drive bad actors out of business. The value of unregulated care is, of course, that it's cut-rate. Without having to meet regulatory standards or invest in quality measures, these providers can charge far less than others. If you're an ALICE parent whose budget is tight as a vise and your choice is between an unregulated provider at $100 a week or a regulated provider at $200 a week, you're picking your poison.

Perversely, the government often feels it can't step in lest it make the problem even worse. Just three years after the death of 20-month-old Kendyll Mire in that Houston childcare, Texas rejected calls to lower the maximum adult-to-child ratio. Why? The Texas Department of Family and Protective Services said, "We have a real fear that if daycare operations must hire more employees to comply with new state mandates, working families with infants and small children may seek out unregulated daycare – and in those settings, children are more likely to be injured, or worse. It is not worth the risk."[127] Similarly, efforts to require mandatory across-the-board licensing tend to be met with the simple objection that providers will respond by closing – and, in fact, experience shows that when licensing requirements rise, a significant number *do* close, just adding to the accessibility crisis.

*   *   *

Bright Spots

We know what public funds can do for formal care because it's the one place where we have some decently funded models. Remember back in the introduction when I mentioned the important exceptions of federally- and state-funded pre-K that's attached to the public school system? It's time to shine a spotlight on the exceptions in order to prove the potential for a rule.

Public school pre-K teachers make by far the highest salary of anyone in the sector, at a median of about $43,000 a year. In three states – Georgia, Alabama, and New Jersey – and a few cities, at least some types of pre-K teachers are part of the same salary table as K-12 teachers.[128] There's a similar story for teachers employed by the Department of Defense (DOD) to provide care to families on military bases.[129]

Unsurprisingly, these teachers stay in their jobs longer and, definitionally, do not need to access significant amounts of public assistance.[130] The improved teacher retention is not a small fact: childcare workers have some of the highest turnover rates of any profession – as an overall average, providers lose close to a third of their staff every year – which should shock exactly no one given the difficulty of the work and the pittance of the pay. Yet unlike turnover in retail or food service, caregiver churn presents a real challenge because of how much relationships matter to young children. It can be confusing and painful for a toddler to grow exceptionally fond of a teacher only to have her abruptly leave. Particularly since most formal care doesn't follow a school-year promotion schedule, this turnover means children may sadly cycle through quite a few teachers before moving to the next classroom[*].

The higher salary for public school pre-K and DOD teachers is generally reflective of higher educational requirements; correlatedly, these programs tend to be of high quality. Similarly, earlier this decade, Head Start, whose teacher salaries fall in between private centers and public school pre-K, phased in a now-met requirement that half of Head Start teachers must have a Bachelor's degree. While Head Start quality varies from program to program, it has on average significant and long-lasting impacts that researchers can detect in high school and beyond.[131] These examples prove that reasonable compensation for childcare teachers is both feasible and desirable.

---

[*] In K-12 education, most teachers who leave choose to exit at the end of the school year, and it matters less to a 5th grader if his 4th grade teacher isn't at the school anymore when he returns from summer break; little kids, on the other hand, usually stay in one class until they reach their next birthday.

What's more, you will never find a public school pre-K or Head Start with conditions like those described in the articles about Deborah Stokes or the Texas centers. Money and oversight can't guarantee high-quality formal care, but it's both a necessary precondition and a quality floor that keeps out those who would harm the most vulnerable among us – a floor that the Credit system would universalize.

Chapter 6: Quality in Informal Care

Home-Based Providers: Caught in the Middle

Step into a home-based group childcare and you're apt to see one adult (the owner-teacher) with six toddlers who aren't potty trained and can each say about, oh, 50 semi-intelligible words.

(When it comes to quality, nannies and au pairs are a distinct set of informal paid providers. Because they're only caring for one or two children, they more closely resemble friends, family & neighbors, so we'll group them into the next chapter.)

Home-based providers are in a tough spot for a category that cares for at least 1.5 million American children each day. They have many of the group care needs of a formal center with chillingly little support. While many home providers are experienced educators with more than a decade of work with children under their belts, they're very often going it alone – in an average state like Minnesota, eight out of ten informal providers have no other adults helping them.[132]

Nor is this a lucrative business. In neighboring Wisconsin, running a home childcare will net you about $7.50 an hour after expenses.[133] For this privilege of barely surviving, home-based providers nationally work an average of 68 hours a week – 55 hours of childcare and 13 hours of administrative work.[134] By themselves. In most cases, it truly is a labor of love and/or a way to bring in a small income while caring for one's own young child, because it's hard to understand why else anyone would choose this path*.

Many informal providers respond with what's honestly logical, if undesirable, under these circumstances: a lot of screen time†. On

---

* Indeed, when surveyed, the most commonly cited motivation home providers give for their work is the enjoyment of caregiving for young children.
† The research on screen time is somewhat mixed, but it is rather clear that if very young children are going to watch screens, it's better to have an adult watching with them and pointing out / conversing about what they're seeing.

average, children in home-based cares watch two to three hours of shows. These are just averages, though, and there are tails on either end; some don't watch any, while one study found a high end of 7 *hours*(!) a day of screen time for some youngsters.[135] On average, informal providers offer significantly lower amounts of literacy- and numeracy-based activities, and there's less time spent on walks or outside at all; only six in ten are reading books every day to their little charges. Most disturbingly, children are significantly more likely to die or suffer abuse (though the absolute numbers remain very low) in unregulated home-based childcares.[136]

Again, though, this isn't to suggest home-based care is fundamentally inferior. It is not. Some parents really value the cozy home environment or having a provider who speaks their language. The smaller group sizes and lack of classroom-to-classroom switching may offer opportunities to build deep and lasting relationships between caregiver and child. Most importantly, this is a structural flaw, not a personal indictment: most of the challenges home providers face are, yet again, because of a lack of funds in the system.

Most glaringly, they can't hire the staff support they need! That's the major risk factor for child injury, not negligence. With only one adult in the house, the odds are just higher of a child getting around a gate and crawling unnoticed towards the stairs while the teacher is changing a diaper. On a more everyday basis, with another set of hands around it's also an awful lot easier to wrangle a bunch of squirmy toddlers into their coats and take them on a walk to the park.

That said, there are existing options for informal providers to improve their quality. Several states, like Indiana and Delaware, offer a modified version of their Quality Rating and Improvement System for family home providers, and there are modified evaluation tools for identifying quality in these settings. Organizations like Child Care Aware of America make available resource toolkits, and some of their state affiliates offer free consultation services. A few localities have fostered partnerships between centers and family homes where master teachers from the centers go to the home-based providers to provide mentorship and support. These are helpful opportunities, but they unfortunately amount to less than a Band-Aid.

That said, I'm not going to shame any parent for using unaccompanied screen time – I know full well that sometimes an hour of Elmo is just necessary for all involved. Everything in moderation.

*   *   *

Home-based care comes in two flavors: lightly regulated and totally unregulated. The trigger for needing to register with the state, as mentioned earlier, is the number of children cared for in the home who are unrelated to the caregiver. Below that threshold, no state inspector will ever show up at your door, no one will ever take note of the quality of your care or even whether you have childproof covers on your electrical outlets. For all intents and purposes, these unregulated informal care providers are off the grid. They form what economists would call a "gray market" – they're unintended and unofficial.[137] Yet the only difference between them and illegal ("black market") providers is that these unregulated providers pay taxes and are 100 percent legal.

Given exceedingly thin profit margins and the potential costs of meeting health and safety regulations, it will not shock you to learn there are about ten times more unregulated than regulated informal providers.[138] Even for the many, many well-intentioned, safe, high-quality informal providers, there's currently every incentive to keep the number of children at or below the trigger threshold for registration and regulation. Remember that these triggers can be eye-raisingly high: South Dakota's 12 children takes the cake, but it is not some rural outlier; a completely middle-of-the-pack state like Missouri allows home providers to serve 8 two-year-olds without regulation.

Even regulated informal providers have oversight that could charitably be considered weak. As the Texas exposé noted, home providers in that state only get inspected once every two years. Initial licensure in a state like Virginia mainly requires ensuring the physical space is in compliance with health and safety standards as well as the conducting of a criminal background check.[139] At least Virginia mandates an in-person inspection prior to license issuance; twelve states don't even require that much.[140]

Again, the perverse incentives rear their head: states have underfunded and overburdened inspection agencies (usually the state Department of Social Services or equivalent) that can't even meet the inspection schedule for the regulated programs they already have. So, they make peace with the raft of unregulated homes. States also know that with so little money in the system, forcing more programs into the regulated light will cause many to close and create an even greater shortage of slots.

* * *

A Revitalized Option

It all comes back to the money. At $15,000 per child, a home-based care could be transformed. First and foremost, they can hire an assistant or two. This would be an adrenaline shot of quality straight to the heart of the subsector. Additionally, through required enrollment in their state's QRIS, there would be vastly more focus on what's actually happening during the day. Home providers would have the breathing room to access the resources available to them. It's reasonable to think that within just a few years, the rates of literacy and numeracy activities, outdoor visits, and so on would come level with formal centers.

Consider the experience that one unregulated home provider wrote about anonymously on a blog.[141] This is a fairly typical informal provider, and keep in mind it's someone who writes that, overall, she enjoys the work:

"As a home daycare provider, you will feel overworked and underpaid. You will have longer hours than the parents whose children you watch because they'll need to drop them off half an hour before work and pick them up half an hour later. Children whose parents work full-time will be in your care about 45 hours a week. You will, however, earn significantly less than those parents working out of the home. Even in areas where childcare rates are higher, you will work more and get paid less than those who work out of the home…

You will be exhausted at the end of the day–maybe even halfway through it. Taking care of your own children is easier than taking care of someone else's. You know your kids and are more in-tune with them. You can also let them run around naked through a cluttered house while you rest on the couch if you like because they are your children. With other people's children, however, you have to get to know them and earn their trust, which takes time. You also can't be as laid-back with them, especially in the supervision department.

You will spend most of your time putting away toys that have been strewn about. You will have to break up little spats, discipline children for hitting or refusing to share and do diaper changes. You'll have to feed everyone snacks and lunch. Rounding everyone up for outings can take time. However, the bulk of your time will be spent making sure it is possible to walk through the playroom. Many states require that you keep toys put away unless they are in use. Parents or inspectors [if you're licensed] could drop in at any time, so you can't be lazy about clutter. Cleaning up messes will also take up a lot more time than discipline or meal-time."

This is someone who clearly feels a commitment to the children she watches, and who understands some basics of child development ("Free play and structured activities will teach the children a lot more than the TV will," she writes elsewhere). It's also someone who is stretched trying to guide the development of a handful of young children all by herself, which isn't a great setup for anyone involved.

Yet herein lies the appeal of informal care: this provider charges $400 a month for full-time care for one child and $600 a month for siblings. Remember that centers can easily cost $1,000 or (significantly) more a month per child, with no sibling discount – this is more than half the cost. With Child Development Credits, this provider would be getting triple her current monthly rate, more than enough to hire at least a part-time assistant. She could focus less on the blocking-and-tackling work of meeting her charges' physical needs and keeping the floors Lego-free, and more on cultivating each child's individual development.

Informal, home-based cares are an important part of the childcare landscape. Right now they're caught between a rock and a hard place; Child Development Credits offer a path back into the open air.

Chapter 7: Quality in Friends, Family, Neighbor (and Nanny) Care

Supporting Grandma

Friend, Family, and Neighbor (FFN) care is literally essential for an enormous number of families. Because it is free, and because of the crippling costs of fee-based care, it is for many truly the only viable form of childcare. As a result, the loss of FFN care can be catastrophic. It's nearly impossible to get an accurate count of FFN providers, but any way you cut it, it's a lot: one estimate puts the national figure at about 2.7 million individuals caring for 4 million young children, close to a fifth of all youngsters.[142]

The archetypal FFN provider is a grandmother, so let's think about what quality means for her. There's no question that grandma is almost always providing a loving, safe environment for her grandchild. As we know, that's unquestionably the top priority. We also know, though, that there may be relatively little engagement beyond that. What limited research exists suggests that all of the lower rates of developmental activities that happen with home-based providers – less reading, more TV – are reflected, at times intensified, in FFN situations.[143]

Now, no one's knocking grandma! Little kids are exhausting; free caregiving may be a labor of love, but it's still labor. I'm a healthy 35-year-old, and Dora the Explorer has been my savior on more than one occasion. What this research shows instead is that grandma needs more information about child development. She may well have grown up in a different era and not understand that just because a baby can't talk, he still needs conversation. She may not think to or know how to turn simple everyday interactions like diaper changes or a walk to the grocery store into brain-building opportunities.

Grandma doesn't need an associate degree in early childhood, but she could use some training. A few cities and states have begun piloting programs in this vein, but they're very small. Nationally, only one in ten FFN caregivers are receiving any ongoing training, and I suspect that number might be generous. It's difficult to find, much less engage, FFN providers, especially with no incentives for participation and no money with which to bring the training programs to scale.

The programs that do exist, though, are promising. Take, for instance, New York City's Caring And Responsive Engagement (C.A.R.E.) program.[144] C.A.R.E offers a series of Saturday workshops to help FFN caregivers, along with 1:1 coaching and other resources. These workshops cover topics ranging from brain development to educational games and activities. In a video produced by the Sesame Street Workshop, you can see C.A.R.E. facilitator Zoraima Rosario-Rolón working with eight caregivers, showing them how a simple act of washing hands after a meal can be a learning opportunity through asking questions like "how does the wipe feel on your hand?" One featured grandmother, Elsa, struggled with the behavior of her grandson; she found herself consistently defaulting to negative responses and admonishments. C.A.R.E. helped her learn positive behavioral interventions, altering the course of her bond with the child and therefore, the child's developmental trajectory.

Across the country is a similar program, the Arizona Kith and Kin Project. This program has been evaluated by researchers and shown to measurably improve caregiver-child interactions, the number of learning activities, and other elements of care that lead to optimal development.[145]

Again, though, we're back to the start: Quality costs money. Right now, these interventions are far from scalable, mainly because they are expensive. C.A.R.E provides that 1:1 coaching as well as $350 in books and other educational materials to each participant. The Arizona project, which has a lighter touch, reaches about 300 caregivers a year; the more intensive C.A.R.E. cohorts are only made up of eight caregivers. If informal caregivers were eligible recipients of the Child Development Credits, however, it would unlock these types of quality training opportunities for the millions of loving relatives, friends, and neighbors who are generously taking young children under their wing.

*   *   *

The Downside of FFN Care

The challenge with completely unregulated providers, particularly those who have no kinship nor 'fictive kinship' (friend-who-might-as-well-be-family) relationship to the child, is that things can go horribly awry and there's no accountability save luck. Elizabeth Gibbons, a professional who moved to Boston with her employed husband and one-year-old in order to attend graduate school, wrote about her harrowing experience for her local NPR affiliate:

"After months of no response from daycare waitlists, we signed up with a budding nanny-share company that facilitated family pairings and offered a slightly lower price than daycare. The guarantees of exceptional care plus a Montessori curriculum lured me in. I could not have imagined the horror to come. The ill-equipped nanny who was placed with our families was overheard swearing at the kids and strapped the other little boy in our share in a high chair in a dark room by himself after hours of crying. After learning of the incidents from our building's concerned maintenance man, I fired her immediately.

That left me with a needy baby in my arms, a mountain of laundry, and a stack of chapters to read for my classes. I panicked as the precarious life balance I'd constructed to go back to school in my mid-30s crumbled. My husband was our sole breadwinner, and our only hope to afford the Boston rent. I wondered if I would have to drop out of school to care for our baby."[146]

While a view of nanny care has been put into the public imagination by movies like *The Nanny Diaries* or *Mary Poppins*, the fact is that nannies are not just utilized by the rich as some form of outsourcing their parenting. Nannies are increasingly used by the middle class, particularly, as Gibbons did, in the form of 'nanny shares' between multiple families.[147] These nanny shares can bring costs down and are often a fallback out of necessity due to the lack of formal or other informal options.

*   *   *

Back to The Basics

WHAT ARE THE BASICS™?

Science shows that 80% of brain growth happens by the age of three! Beginning from birth, young brains develop like little muscles, getting bigger and stronger the more you and your family interact with your child.

The Basics are five fun, simple, and powerful ways to help all our children aged 0-3 grow to be happy and smart.

Do all of the Basics every day to help your child
become the amazing person you know they can be.

 ### Maximize Love, Manage Stress

Babies and toddlers thrive when their world feels loving, safe, and predictable. Respond with smiles, words, and touch to help them see, hear, and feel your love. You will help them develop a sense of security and self-control.

 ### Talk, Sing, and Point

Babies learn language from the moment they are born. Respond to their sounds, and later, their words. Connect with eye contact and a loving tone of voice, while pointing to help them know what you are talking about.

 ### Count, Group, and Compare

Every child's brain is wired for math. Talk about numbers, shapes, patterns, and comparisons as you go about your routines together. Watch your child learn to love math.

 ### Explore Through Movement and Play

Babies are like scientists who love making discoveries. Watch to see what interests your child, then encourage their curiosity and help them learn when they play and explore.

 ### Read and Discuss Stories

Reading turns kids into confident thinkers. Make books a regular part of your relationship from the very beginning. With infants, point at the pictures and speak with excitement. With toddlers, just make it fun.

Who Is Involved?

Lots of people! Partners include hospitals, health centers, schools, community centers, childcare providers, churches, family members, and others.

What If I'm Not a Parent?

You still care about children! Learn about the Basics. Encourage parents and caregivers to make sure their children experience all five with everyone who cares for them.

How Can I Learn More?

Visit www.thebasics.org or connect with us on social media for information on the campaign, opportunities in your community, tips, and videos.

Created by the Achievement Gap Initiative at Harvard University, fueled by The Basics, Inc., a network of organizations, and local campaigns in the Basics Learning Network.
© 2016 President and Fellows of Harvard College

 The Basics

www.TheBasics.org

Child Development Credits could transform what FFN care looks like in similar ways as home-based informal providers, but for different reasons. Home-based providers could use the funds to hire an assistant. FFN providers and nannies could use the funds to get trained.

Perhaps this training should simply be in what Harvard University scholar Ron Ferguson has distilled into a five-point program called, appropriately, "The Basics"* (see the accompanying image for more detail):

> ➢ Maximize love, manage stress
> ➢ Talk, sing, and point
> ➢ Count, group, and compare
> ➢ Explore through movement and play
> ➢ Read and discuss stories

These elements of The Basics are all ways to enhance everyday interactions with children in ways that are proven to promote their healthy development. An immigrant neighbor who only speaks Spanish can just as easily follow The Basics as a rural grandmother or a wealthy family's au pair.

Requiring that every FFN provider and nanny get a baseline level of training to be eligible for the Credits seems only reasonable. Recall the low-quality, low-cost nanny that the Copelands were considering. The choice should never have to be between holistic quality and mere safety. The Credits would ensure that all FFN providers, as well as nannies, know enough about child development to do both.

---

* The program, piloted in Boston, includes numerous parent-friendly resources like videos and handouts, and is currently available in English and Spanish. For more, see www.TheBasics.org.

Chapter 8: Quality in Parental Care

Parental Stress

When I stayed home for six weeks with my eldest daughter when she was an infant, I marveled at how an 11-pound creature who didn't yet understand she had arms could leave me so thoroughly bemused and bewildered. All parents could certainly benefit from access to more resources like workshops, or perhaps magic potions that make babies sleep through the night. However, for parents – especially stay-at-home parents – the money-quality connection shows itself foremost in the first element of The Basics: Maximize love, manage stress.

There is a significant body of research that shows parental stress can have a negative and lasting impact on children.[148] It's the shadow side of attachment theory – highly stressed-out parents are likely to be unpredictable or non-attentive, and this leads to insecure attachments among youngsters, which starts a negative cascade. At worst, epic levels of ongoing stress can spike the risk for neglect, abuse, divorce, or other traumatic events that make up a category researchers call Adverse Childhood Experiences, or ACEs.[149]

Stress can also impact babies before they're born – the stress levels in both parents' bodies pre-conception, and in the mother's body during pregnancy, influence fetal development. As explained by Dr. Michael C. Lu, former Director of the U.S. Department of Health and Human Services' Maternal and Child Health Bureau, it's an evolutionary way for fetal brains to know whether they're preparing to enter a harmonious environment or a dangerous one.[150] So, while we don't want any caregivers highly stressed, it takes on special importance among parents because of their unique emotional and physiological bonds with children.

Before the parents reading this start sweating with shame, please know that what we're talking about here is *sustained, high-level stress* – "toxic stress".[151] This is not about the occasional day you (and I) lose our head and scream at your (my) kid because you're on edge thanks to a big project at work or the car starting to make a disturbing clunking sound. The classic neuroscience truism is that neurons which "fire together, wire together" – in other words, our brains learn through repetition after repetition after repetition. There are also two pieces of good news: first, as we saw in Section I, the brains of young children are very malleable and can quickly recover if their circumstances are changed; and second, the presence of other stable, loving adults can act as a buffer against toxic stress. Harvard's Center on the Developing Child is very specific about the definition of toxic stress: "Prolonged activation of the stress response system in the absence of protective relationships."

Still, the best and easiest way to avoid toxic stress is to support parents. If Mom is generally warm and loving and safe, a child's brain can easily absorb a bad day ("rupture and repair," in scientific parlance; with secure attachment, the brain is "buffered"). However, if a parent is cycling through chronic stress-related depression and anger, the child's brain gets confused: it's unclear if adults are safe, it's unclear if needs will be met. This insecure attachment can lead to maladaptive behaviors – logical but unhelpful – like acting up (throwing a tantrum or a chair) to get attention, or withdrawal (why bother asserting a need if it won't be met?).

I want to say explicitly, by the way, that these parents do not love their children one iota less than anyone else, nor are ACEs deterministic. Toxic stress is a health condition; as we all know from times in our lives we've been acutely stressed, a brain overflooded with cortisol has an extraordinarily powerful gravitational pull against our better angels. Also, many stressed-out parents were themselves recipients of ACEs, which leave both scars and heightened risk factors; another truism is that even among infants and toddlers whose long-term memory hasn't yet kicked in, "the body remembers."[*]

It's also fairly obvious that highly stressed-out caregivers are less likely to follow the other Basics. For one thing, stress leads to poor sleep, just what parents getting up three times a night with the baby need. For

---

[*] For more on this topic, I strongly recommend California Surgeon General Dr. Nadine Burke-Harris' book *The Deepest Well: Healing the Long-Term Effects of Childhood Adversity*.

another, when you're in a near-permanent state of fight-or-flight-or-freeze – when you're in a scarcity mindset and your brain is literally narrowing your focus to survival essentials – it's tough to have the patience and attention needed to read picture books, do counting activities, or even just get on the floor and play. Stress also puts tremendous strain on marriages and other partnering relationships, threatening the stability of the entire family unit.

So why does money matter so much here? Because financial problems are the genesis of so, so much stress, both the toxic kind described above and more moderate versions. According to the American Psychological Association, money is the undisputed champion of stress – it's consistently found to be the number one stress generator among Americans.[152] One study showed that simply putting people into a *make-believe* state of financial stress – asking them to imagine that their car broke down and they needed to come up with two grand for repairs – reduced their performance on cognitive tests equal to as if they had missed an entire night's sleep.[153] Recall that the Centers for Disease Control lists enhancing financial security as one of the top five strategies for preventing child abuse and neglect; this is why[*].[154]

The group most likely to experience fiscal stress? Parents. In a 2014 survey, more than three-quarters of parents, a full 77 percent, reported money being a "somewhat" or "very" significant source of stress. Across all Americans, nearly a quarter reported experiencing "extreme" money stress in the past month. As we've seen throughout this book, these financial stressors are most assuredly not isolated to people living below the poverty line. There can be no question that this stress is negatively impacting both parents and their parenting. As the Pew Research Center puts it, "a broad, demographically based look at the landscape of American families reveals stark parenting divides linked less to philosophies or values and more to economic circumstances and changing family structure [divorce, etc.]."[155]

The best thing we can do for parents, then, is let them be parents. For instance, compensating stay-at-home parents isn't going to solve every financial difficulty, but it puts some slack back on the line. $15,000 is

---

[*] The other four top strategies: change social norms to support parents and positive parenting; provide quality care and education early in life; enhance parenting skills to promote healthy child development; and intervene to lessen harms and prevent future risk.

mental breathing room. It's space to be able to curse the bad luck of the car's battery dying but then playing peek-a-boo with your baby while you wait for the mechanic to call back. It's being able to chat with your toddler about the different fruits and vegetables in the produce aisle instead of anxiously worrying whether getting the tomatoes *and* the spinach will overdraw your account. Put bluntly, Child Development Credits are likely, on average, to improve everyone's parenting.

That, of course, includes the parenting of families with all parents in the workforce. Zeroing out childcare expenses frees up that money to be used elsewhere, the equivalent of a cash transfer with equivalent stress-reducing impacts. Beyond the direct impacts on parent-child interactions, reducing stress also improves the strength and satisfaction of partnering relationships such as marriages, which, as we've seen, form the heart of the child development ecosystem.[156] Put another way, a feeling of plenty promotes relational health in all directions. There's a reason those studies find that even modestly upping a family's income has tremendous positive benefits across the board in terms of education, health, and happiness.

Remember, even when children are spending many hours in non-parental care, the bulk of their weeks are still spent at home. In fact, studies have borne out that parenting quality has an outsized impact on child development regardless of whether the child is in a regular external care environment. Researchers don't yet know exactly why this is the case, but as Emily Oster writes, one theory is that children are hypersensitive to the powerful consistency of the bond with their parents/guardians.[157]

The need to destress parents is perhaps more important today than ever before. In the current era – despite the increases in dual-worker households and non-traditional work hours, to say nothing of the rise of the 'side hustle' or 'gig economy' – parents still somehow manage to spend *more* time with their children than in previous generations. In fact, a *New York Times* article aptly titled *The Relentlessness of Modern Parenting* noted that research shows modern working mothers "spend just as much time tending their children as stay-at-home mothers did in the 1970s."[*][158]

---

[*] There's also been a tremendous increase in fathers' average hours of active participation in parenting, not that us dads particularly need a pat on the back for finally jogging onto the field.

In the end, a lot of this comes back to the fact that brain development is a hard worker. It doesn't limit itself to a nine-to-five schedule, it doesn't take weekends or holidays off, it doesn't particularly care whether parents work during the day or not, and it's definitely paying attention to the overall warmth or coldness of the child-parent relationship.

*　*　*

Helping a Parent Out

The other thing that stabilizing parents' financial situation does is let them get some help. Stay-at-home parents could especially use that help: recall Ruth Watt's story of crying by the tomatoes while still recovering from childbirth. It's a plain fact that being a stay-at-home parent has pretty awful fringe benefits: there are no holidays, no sick leave[†]. They don't even get a lunch hour unless the kids' nap schedules magically line up and they actually go to sleep. With squeezed budgets, the luxury of getting a babysitter or dropping the kids at the local YMCA is often a pipe dream; among several women I talked to, including Ruth, babysitters were mainly for necessities, like watching the kids so that the caregiving parent could finally go to the doctor for a cough that won't quit. The Credits could also help with the "people problem" that Ruth talked about; as mentioned earlier, there would likely be a rise in communal spaces designed for young children, like Finland's "open centers," where stay-at-home parents, FFN caregivers, and informal providers could regularly meet up[‡].

There are also more intensive forms of parental support that would be unlocked. Our eldest daughter was an incredibly difficult infant, even

---

[†] Short of a partner or pal taking over the caregiving to give the stay-at-home parent a break, which often isn't feasible; and even when it is, resting while the toddler screams downstairs or bangs on the bedroom door is a very generous definition of a break.

[‡] In sociological terms, these groups of caregivers currently tend a lack a "second place" in terms of their social environment. As coined by Ray Oldenburg, the "first place" is the home, the "second place" is the workplace, and the "third place" is a relaxing communal space frequented by friends (e.g. a church, a bar). For stay-at-home parents, their home is their workplace, hence the increased isolation. We'd do well to be more deliberate about providing opportunities for caregivers to access an external "second place" (and more family-friendly "third places," for that matter).

by infant standards – she would wail for an hour or more every evening before settling into a fitful sleep; nighttime became wartime. We were privileged enough to have the fiscal resources to hire a baby consultant of sorts who helped provide both reassurance and practical tips that made the nights manageable. Other couples we know have been kept sane (I use that word meaningfully*) by having a postpartum doula or a night nanny providing bridge support during the first chaotic weeks and months. There's an entire subfield of trained professionals known as 'home visitors' whose entire job is to support families with young children by offering individualized help.

All families deserve these supports because they are an absolute good for all involved. A mom who can focus on recovering from the truly epic and heroic work of birthing a child is a mom who is more likely to be able to form a secure bond; with another set of non-sleep-deprived hands nearby, it's also more likely that challenges like postpartum depression will be caught and addressed early.

Again, a thriving family leads to a thriving child.

None of these services, though, are – or should be – cheap. The services of providers like a postpartum doula can run into the high hundreds of dollars, and home visiting programs (usually run by government or nonprofit organizations) have per-client price tags in the high thousands. Yet the benefits are enormous: rigorous studies have found that home visiting leads to big reductions in things like pregnancy-induced hypertension, preterm births, and emergency room visits due to child injuries – all of which are factors that inarguably impact the well-being of mothers, babies, and entire families.[159]

Yet relatively few women have access to these needed supports. Formal home visiting programs have some federal funding, yet for instance, in my Richmond region, only about one in ten eligible women get home visiting services due to a lack of supply†. Similarly, although doulas are rising in popularity, less than one in ten women currently utilize them, and those that do are more likely to be affluent.[160] By paying stay-at-home parents and zeroing out the external childcare costs

---

* Mothers' mental health is serious business. According to data from the nonprofits Zero To Three and ChildTrends, 22 percent of moms of infants and toddlers "rate their mental health as worse than 'excellent' or 'very good'."

† These formal home visiting programs, supported by federal Maternal, Infant, and Early Childhood Home Visiting (MIECHV) grants, are specifically targeted at lower-income families.

for working parents, we would provide vastly greater access to hands-on supports, setting in motion a positive cascade that reduces stress, improves parenting, and generally leads to happier and healthier homes.

SECTION III: MAKING THE CHANGE

Chapter 9: Childcare Should Be a Bipartisan Issue

Strange Political Bedfellows

You'd be hard-pressed to find more politically different leaders than Rick Santorum and George Miller. Santorum is the arch-conservative former Pennsylvania Senator and two-time GOP presidential candidate, coming in second to Mitt Romney for the nomination in 2012. Miller, less widely known, is a liberal lion; the former longtime Democratic Congressman from the San Francisco Bay Area had his hand in nearly every major piece of legislation over the past four decades.

These two gentlemen don't agree on a lot. They agree that childcare costs too much.

In a June 2018 *Roll Call* op-ed they co-authored through the Bipartisan Policy Center, Santorum and Miller wrote that:

"For millions of parents juggling low-wage jobs, it's a daily struggle to provide the basics, from housing and food to adequate medical care, let alone to afford high-quality childcare. In many cases, these pressures and stresses are most acute just at the time when children are going through critical periods of cognitive and emotional development — years that lay the foundation for later learning and career success.

The good news is that [a] survey, conducted for the Bipartisan Policy Center, [found] broad support for efforts to ensure that all children get a strong start in life.

By wide margins, liberal and conservative respondents alike expressed concern about the high cost of quality childcare; agreed that many parents have too little time to spend with their children; felt that all children should be guaranteed the shelter, food, education, and care needed to thrive; and supported programs to help childcare workers earn a living wage. Importantly, a majority said they would be willing to pay higher taxes for programs that help children, even if those programs don't directly benefit them."[161]

The politics of childcare affordability, accessibility, and quality are shockingly good, particularly for this hyperpolarized political environment. A separate poll in 2016 found that 82 percent of Republicans, 86 percent of Independent and 98 percent of Democrats agreed that "making early education and childcare more affordable for working families to give children a strong start" should be a national priority.[162] The reason should be fairly clear by now: the issue doesn't know ideological or geographic boundaries. Suburban Republican women, 'Left Coast' city-dwellers, rural heartlanders – everyone has to deal with childcare*. That said, the angles of approach vary by political affiliation. Santorum and Miller continue:

"Of course, conservative and liberal views on these topics differ. For example, conservatives are less likely to say that government has a primary responsibility to support early childhood development, are more concerned that government will overstep its role, and place a greater emphasis on parental involvement and teaching values in early childhood programs. Liberals, by contrast, see a greater role for government but are concerned that public programs will be ineffective or inefficient, and tend to prioritize academic and developmental foundations."

This chapter will delve deeper into the respective conservative and liberal cases for universal childcare. Then we'll look at the practicalities of what a bipartisan movement could look like.

Although on some level it may feel like this should be a

---

* Even Congress needs childcare: Recently, the U.S. House of Representatives (under Republican control at the time) spent $12 million of taxpayer funds to build a state-of-the-art center adjacent to the Capitol. The center is exclusively for the children of House employees, who get a discounted rate. The perfectly reasonable goal is to attract and retain talented staff, which shows that on some level, Congressional leaders understand the work-childcare connection.

straightforward movement to build, the politics of childcare are complicated. Writing in 1976, just a few years after President Nixon's veto of the 1971 Comprehensive Child Development Act, scholar William Roth wrote that:

"To understand the prospects for future legislation providing for childcare it must be first understood that a concern for children is but one of the concerns that motivates childcare legislation – it frequently is not even the most important. It was not the most important motivation behind the Comprehensive Child Development Act, nor did the concern prevent the veto of that Act. Historically, childcare has been part of an overall strategy, either permitting or encouraging women to work. The current interest in childcare did not spring from the wish of middle-class women to participate in the workforce. Rather it started as a way to ensure that poor women could labor at jobs the richer women would have disdained. Neither did childcare sprout from women's liberation, but it did develop from the need to have poor women work— the government gets the benefit of their work as well as relief from the liability of welfare payments. This is the tradition of childcare.

...What moves political action is considerably more complex than thinking that children are important enough to warrant political consideration; deciding to implement policy on behalf of children, and following through with political action to implement that policy; the connection of politics to policy is far richer than that. There are always many things to motivate a political actor. Only one of these things is an immediate concern for the issue at hand, and even this concern is frequently embedded in other issues such as ideology and concern for others represented."[163]

We do have one thing going for us today that advocates didn't have in the early 1970s, bitter as the taste may be: the state of childcare has gotten so very bad – and the impacts felt across so very many income brackets* – that every constituency, interest group, and political party has reason to get behind a fix.

---

* Recall that in the early 1970s, well less than half of U.S. households had both parents working, and those families were heavily concentrated at the lower income levels.

*   *   *

Making the Conservative Case

I am not a conservative by any stretch of the imagination; I was actually voted "most liberal" in my 400-person high school graduating class. That said, I have a healthy respect for conservative perspectives. My early career was spent in what would be termed the 'education reform movement,' historically a broad coalition of civil rights-focused groups on the Left and business-focused groups on the Right aiming to improve school outcomes for all students.

There are, of course, significant overlaps in 'conservative values' and 'liberal values' – everyone wants the best for their children, as one obvious example. Yet it's undeniable that different values influence different political viewpoints. Social psychologist Jonathan Haidt's research shows that conservatives and liberals have what he terms different "moral taste buds," a palate made up of the same basic values (things like respect for authority or a desire to stop harm) but with distinct responses to social issues, much like cultures with different tolerances for spicy food.[164]

With that framing in mind, the conservative case for Child and Youth Development Credits is, in no particular order, five-pronged:

First, it's a strongly pro-family policy. It enables families to have more children instead of having childcare concerns artificially cap family size. It also enables families to have more quality time together. This does not just apply to families where parents are working multiple jobs to make ends meet, and definitionally have less time available for a family meal. Childcare cost burdens are huge contributors to making most parents feel, in the words of a Pew survey, "stressed, tired, and rushed," the state in which modern parents often exist day after day (ten million parents of youngsters are currently nodding their heads vigorously in agreement).[165]

Indeed, recall that stress can be the main barrier to a healthy parent-child relationship; though this isn't a parenting book, it's relevant that nearly every study has found that for most ages, the *quality* of family time matters far more than the quantity.[166] Yet stress and quality time are nearly incompatible because quality time requires presence, not a worrying mind. Building in financial 'slack' and reducing stress has rippling impacts that creates buffers. And, as mentioned earlier, family stress not only negatively affects children, it's a major contributor to our sky-high divorce rates.[167]

Compensating stay-at-home parents also goes to the heart of family matters, as a majority of conservatives would prefer mothers to be home with the children in the early years. Since so many women are heading into the workforce by necessity and not choice, providing income for caregiving can bolster what are often seen as faltering family dynamics. I'm not projecting here; a 2017 article in *The American Conservative* titled "Why Not Pay Women to Stay Home, Raise Children?" directly offered the case that "if the family really is the bedrock of society, how can we not do everything possible to promote its growth and stave off its dissolution?"[168]

Additionally – and some conservatives would likely say this reason should go first – making childcare free will reduce abortions. Setting *entirely* to the side the moral debate around abortion, it is a fact that serious concerns about the costs of childrearing influence a significant number of women's choice to terminate an unplanned pregnancy.[169] In some surveys of women who have abortions, financial fears are the single most commonly cited influence. When you allay those concerns, fewer women may choose abortion (I'm hardly the first to make this point, by the way – in 2017, conservative analyst Patrick T. Brown penned a *Washington Post* op-ed in the runup to the March For Life entitled "Want to reduce abortion rates? Give parents money."[170]). This has actually been borne out in practice: in 2007, when Spain initiated a modest, one-time cash child allowance, their monthly abortion rate saw a nearly-instantaneous 5 percent drop[*].[171] Imagine the reduction impact from a full Child Development Credit system.

Second, it's a choice-based program. As the Santorum-Miller op-ed notes, conservatives are more likely to see childrearing as the inviolable sanctum of the parents. Indeed, a general distrust of government intervention in this realm has been behind pockets of conservative opposition to public pre-K programs. Nixon's 1971 veto still echoed in 2016 when the official Republican National Committee platform was

---

[*] Immediately after giving birth, Spanish mothers received a one-time unconditional payment of the equivalent of $3,800.

nearly amended to oppose government-run pre-K because, in words of one Committee member, it "inserts the state in the family relationship in the very early stages of a child's life."[172] Though the amendment didn't pass, the adopted GOP platform was quite explicit that the party takes as a core precept that "parents have a right to direct their children's education, care, and upbringing."[173]

This bedrock belief in parental agency animates conservative support for charter schools, private school vouchers, and other forms of K-12 school choice. As mentioned earlier, this is the political reason that I believe a movement for a Quebec-style childcare system is likely to falter. Instead, the Credit system puts the power squarely in parents' hands. This choice would be relatively unfettered (quality guardrails aside), including allowing the Credits to be used at religiously-based providers.

What's more, since the Credits will power a functional marketplace, it allows market forces rather than government edicts to shape the landscape of offerings. This should generate a positive pressure for increasing the quality of care while limiting heavy-handed government intervention.

Third, this is a pro-work policy. Conservatives have a strong belief in the vital importance and dignity of work. Yet we know that childcare is a tremendous barrier for those who wish to work, and for those who are working, a tremendous barrier to advancing up the socioeconomic ladder through their effort. Recall that nearly two million individuals a year either quit a job, don't take a job, or greatly change their job as a result of childcare challenges. If one truly believes that America is a meritocracy – that when you follow the rules, work hard, follow the 'success sequence', you should move up that ladder – then free childcare is a prerequisite.

Free childcare is also a giant boost for the middle class. The vital American worker is currently the one who is being booted off the ladder through no fault of his or her own. Electricians, farmers, truck drivers, manufacturers, machinists, teachers, nurses – these are the types of occupations that make the American economy turn. Yet these are also middle-income occupations where families are being stepped on (mainly, I'd argue, by extractive corporations) until they are barely clinging, one emergency away from slipping off altogether. Zero out childcare costs, and suddenly there's room to grab hold again and resume the ascent.

At the same time, it's also a way to help poor people help themselves. In a family where parents are doing everything society expects and more – working multiple jobs, saving up, being good citizens – all it takes is a single childcare breakdown to put them back at square one. The neighbor who has been watching the kid for an affordable fee abruptly falls ill, which leads to a few missed days of work, which leads to being fired, which leads to falling behind on the rent, which leads to eviction – and suddenly the family that's doing everything right has spun out into complete crisis.

If work is key, then would-be workers must be allowed to work.

Fourth, free childcare is pro-business. Not only does it stabilize and grow the already $40 billion childcare sector itself, but it is hugely important for companies nationwide both for their current and future workforces. As the U.S. Chamber of Commerce report cited in the first chapter noted, every year, childcare breakdowns are causing the loss of billions of dollars in productivity.[174] Because of the ragged state of the childcare marketplace, only a tiny number of as-needed drop-in centers or other forms of backup care exist*. Childcare challenges also cause heightened rates of employee turnover and create difficulties with finding qualified workers, particularly for companies situated in childcare deserts. Increasingly, some larger companies like Patagonia, Nike, and Home Depot are turning towards creating their own on-site childcare centers (at corporate headquarters) because they've realized the economic return on investment, but this is obviously not a sustainable solution for most businesses.

What's more, the critically important nature of the earliest years means that high-quality childcare is helping build the brains of the next generation of workers. The Chamber report puts it plainly: "High-quality care advances children's early development, helping them build a range of critical skills necessary for their success in school and beyond. On the other hand, low-quality early environments, lacking adequate cognitive and noncognitive stimulation, lead to deficits that children often never overcome."

---

* In early 2019, a group of moms who work at Amazon (self-described "Momazonians") made the news for starting a push for a backup care benefit at the commercial giant.

The world is changing, and more than ever, American businesses need workers who can bring a full suite of hard and soft skills to bear in order to creatively and collaboratively solve problems. So do our nation's armed forces, making early childhood a national security issue. Mike Petters, CEO of Huntington Ingalls Industries, America's largest military shipbuilder, is an early childhood champion partially because he can clearly see these linkages. Petters said in a 2015 speech:

"A couple of years ago, I was at a conference being addressed by the Secretary of the Navy. He asked us to consider the U.S. population between the ages of 18 and 25. Now remove from that group those with criminal records, those with physical fitness issues and those without high school diplomas, and you're left with about 25 percent of that population. That is who the Navy is trying to recruit. As I sat there, I thought: Me too.

One in four is a staggering indictment. Now take that to a fifth-grade classroom. One in four students in that classroom will ultimately be employable. The other three will face challenges that we all will pay for."[175]

Put simply, today's toddlers become tomorrow's job applicants within the blink of an economy's eye.

Fifth, Child and Youth Development Credits are an efficient way to streamline government bureaucracy. Right now, government intervention in the first five years is a patchwork of subsidies (both through the Child Care and Development Fund and the Temporary Assistance for Needy Families program), tax breaks, Head Start, state pre-K, Title I pre-K, and so on. These funding streams and offerings often flow through a half-dozen or more agencies by the time they reach the family they're designed to help. Instead of this morass of siloed programs, streamlining government funding for childcare into a relatively simple Credit system would reduce the government's overall footprint in early childhood. If there's one thing everyone agrees the government is good at, it's cutting checks; you can complain about a lot when it comes to government, but social security checks always arrive on time.

Pro-family. Choice-based. Pro-work. Pro-business. Efficient. Child Development Credits should light up conservatives' moral taste buds.

* * *

Making the Liberal Case

The liberal case for free childcare is a bit more straightforward because there's less instinctive resistance to the idea of a large-scale social program. Indeed, if anything, liberals tend to want their leaders to be more vocally out in front on this issue – as a 2019 *New York Times* op-ed by left-leaning pundit Katha Pollitt put it, universal childcare should be "on the front burner of the revitalized left."[176] That said, the liberal case can be made with five pillars of its own:

First, it's a massive anti-poverty move. A third of young children live in families with an annual income of $40,000 or less. From a family support standpoint, zeroing out childcare costs saves them thousands of crucial dollars a year. For a poor family that currently uses relatively cheap informal care at say, $3,000 a year, that's suddenly money that can be used to acquire stable housing or to put into savings so that the next time the car gets a flat tire, it's an inconvenience and not a catastrophe.

What's more, the fact that Credits can be utilized to secure more reliable care than the shaky informal network many lower-income parents are forced to use is a boon for family's prospects. Contrary to popular belief, the vast majority of poor people are not persistently, permanently poor; they bob in and out of poverty as they cycle through getting a job and random events that cause them to lose it.[177] Since we know that childcare breakdowns are a major source of losing shift jobs, or being unable to take a better position that doesn't work logistically with care, settling the care question sturdies the ladder.

From a school readiness standpoint, simultaneously providing high-quality care at scale while increasing family means is, as we've seen, a game-changer. Early childhood gaps will shrink dramatically, and vastly more children will arrive at kindergarten ready to go, while the Youth Development Credits will help ensure they don't fall behind once there. Schools will be freer to focus on the core work of teaching and learning.

Education is often talked about as the silver bullet for breaking the cycle of poverty. In one sense, it is: getting a college degree is, on the whole, a ticket to better earnings in careers with more benefits and upward mobility, yet only about 1 in 10 poor kids end up graduating college.[178] On the other hand, schools and education are not synonyms; in-school factors like teachers can only explain about a third of the puzzle of a student's academic achievement. Most of the rest comes from out-of-school factors like the home environment, which reliably outweigh in-school factors (plus some is a black box of randomness we can't quite yet explain).[179]

This makes sense because learning happens in the brain, and as we've seen, brains under chronic stress and poverty are not well primed to learn. Making childcare free for families is a direct, twofold educational intervention: Higher-quality providers do a better job building the foundations of literacy and numeracy while reducing family stress, allowing healthy brain development and ensures children can bring their fullest selves to the learning process.

Second, it supports equity goals. The populations with the least access to high-quality childcare – and yet arguably the populations that most need access to overcome systemic barriers – are disproportionately people of color and people with lower incomes. Yet a recent analysis from the nonprofit CLASP has shown only 8 percent(!) of eligible children currently receive federal childcare subsidies, and there is significant variation by race and state of residence.[180]

Moreover, a recurring theme in this book is that the childcare burden tends to fall squarely on women's shoulders. Mothers are more often the ones who end up severely altering their work situations or leaving the workforce altogether out of necessity and not choice. Recall the mother in chapter two who had to leave her dream job because the dollars and cents just didn't make sense anymore. The rise in maternal employment that follows increases in publicly-supported childcare is proof that many women's choices are being constrained.

Similarly, paying stay-at-home parents (who are also overwhelmingly women) is an idea with feminist underpinnings. Women have long performed uncompensated domestic labor, which has all sorts of symbolic and practical implications for how our society sees the role and status of women. This disconnect eventually gave rise to the Wages for Housework movement in the mid-1970s.[181] This is an opportunity to finally provide stay-at-home mothers with the dignity they've long been denied. Indeed, the vein of gender runs deeply through this mine; if one parent is fiscally forced to stay home, it's usually the mother, and thus as Pollitt put it in her op-ed, "Lack of childcare also promotes the less quantifiable but real tendency of parenthood to turn previously egalitarian couples into gender stereotypes."

Third, providing robust Credits ensures that early childhood teachers (who are, to continue the previous point, close to 100 percent female and highly racially diverse) are treated with the respect they deserve. Cultivating the brain development of little children, while also attending to their physical needs, is incredibly demanding work. I am exhausted after a day with only my two young children, much less a classroom full of them. While America's public school teachers are certainly not paid enough, they at least make a living wage with reasonable benefits like health insurance and paid time off. Paying early childhood teachers what we pay parking lot attendants is as insulting as it is unsustainable.

Fourth, the positive impacts of free childcare will cascade through other social issues. More children in high-quality programs means more chances for early developmental screenings that can catch things like vision or speech issues early. Reducing family stress will literally make people healthier, as chronic stress spikes an individual's risk for a whole host of medical conditions. The educational benefits are difficult to overstate. And, as noted above, it creates a virtuous cycle where more available income leads to better housing and all the other conditions that allow for self-sufficiency.

Fifth, perhaps more philosophically, free childcare will drastically increase the number of families that are thriving, not just surviving. Vibrant young families are the lifeblood of communities. Parents, as we'll talk about in an upcoming chapter, are inherently more likely to be advocates for green space, clean air, safe streets, and communal events. Having little ones running around reframes a community's self-interest from one of immediacy to a long-term view (I'm reminded of the Native American aphorism that we merely "borrow the Earth from our children"). When families turn insular because their entire capacity is taken up with making it through one week at a time, they cannot fully engage civically or communally. Families may also engage less because as things stand, they're just less happy. Research shows that both mothers and fathers in the U.S. experience the highest "happiness penalty" of any developed nation; yet the hit to happiness isn't due to American kids waking up at 5:00am while Swiss kids magically sleep in, it's "entirely explained by the presence or absence of social policies that allow parents to better combine paid work with family obligations."[182] Finally, when couples start curtailing the number of children they have because childcare concerns are causing a constant struggle, we risk societal atrophy. Free childcare is a path to a more positive future.

*　　*　　*

There are, of course, parts of the concept that each side won't love. Perhaps most galling for conservatives, they'll need to swallow tax increases, even if the Credits quickly pay for themselves. For liberals, they'll have to get OK with a voucher-like system that includes religious providers and perhaps less oversight than they'd want. One more time for those in the back, Bismarck!: politics is the art of the possible, the attainable, the next best. While it's imperfect, universal free childcare is politically viable – something precious few major social change proposals can say at the moment.

Politics is compromise.

*　　*　　*

Building a Movement

So what would a burgeoning bipartisan movement for Child and Youth Development Credits look like? The foundation would be a powerhouse one-two punch of parents and business leaders. Civil rights groups, women's equality groups, and organized labor could bolster the case from the left, with family-values and religious conservatives joining from the right. While this might seem like an unlikely coalition, there is a somewhat uncomfortable truism in politics first spoken by Henry Kissinger: There are no permanent friends and no permanent enemies – only permanent interests. Universal childcare merges the interests of diverse groups like a rare planetary alignment.

On the parental side, there are few more unassailable messengers than young moms and dads. The early childhood advocacy group Zero to Three organizes an annual event in Washington, D.C. and state capitals endearingly called "Strolling Thunder™" (a riff off veterans groups' Rolling Thunder event). Instead of thousands of vets on motorcycles rumbling towards the Capitol on Memorial Day, Strolling Thunder involves hundreds of young parents with their infants and toddlers in tow. The demonstration is designed to raise awareness of issues impacting young families and regularly draws in high-profile speakers from both parties.[183] Lawmakers who met with parents during the 2018 Strolling Thunder event included Senate Minority Leader Chuck Schumer (D-NY) and then-Rep. Ileana Ros-Lethinen (R-FL).

However, with only meager solutions to the care crisis currently on the table, Strolling Thunder and similar organizing efforts are more a distant rumble than a mighty storm. A bold idea like free childcare can be a rallying cry that brings more groups into the fold. Imagine a coalition spanning from Christian conservative group One Million Moms to liberal activist group Moms Rising. Imagine Strolling Thunder times a thousand, with scores of young parents filling the National Mall and the grounds of statehouses across America. What politician wants to stand up, look at those faces and those cameras, and say "no"?

What's more, childcare offers a unique opportunity to rally advocates from across issue areas. There are few other topics that should gather the attention and energy of everyone from education reformers to pro-life activists to Medicare-for-All backers to business leaders to climate warriors.

Take those who work in higher education as an example. Higher education is a massive sector with over half a trillion dollars in annual expenditures.[184] In recent years, higher education leaders have been wringing their hands over low completion rates. Stunningly few students (especially low-income students) finish their degrees, and it's a particularly pronounced problem at community colleges, where nearly one-in-two drop out before completing. Yet as Temple University's Sara Goldrick-Rab and others have shown, a huge contributing factor to non-completion comes down to basic needs, like not having enough food, housing, or, you guessed it, childcare.

Fully 22 percent of college students are parents, and the childcare crisis is written in their statistics: whereas roughly half of all students across two- and four-year institutions complete their degree, less than a third of student parents do.[185] A report from the Institute for Women's Policy Research put it succinctly: "Research has shown that, for many parents who leave school without earning a credential, better access to childcare could have helped them avoid taking a break or dropping out completely."

Alternatively, consider the amount of dollars, breath, time, energy, and digital ink spent fighting over issues like K-12 public charter schools. In the 2018 race for California State Superintendent of Education (a mostly ceremonial position!), the two candidates – whose race, as one article said, became a "proxy war between California's teachers unions and wealthy charter school advocates" – drew in over $61 million.[186] That single contest approaches the combined annual budgets of Child Care Aware of America and the National Association for the Education of Young Children, two of the major U.S. groups representing the interests of young families. This fact says something especially considering that free, high-quality childcare in the birth-to-five years would do more for educational attainment in this country than perhaps any other single policy.

Universal childcare is a college completion policy.

Universal childcare is a K-12 education policy.

Universal childcare is a health care policy.

Universal childcare is an anti-poverty policy.

Universal childcare is a business growth policy.

The sheer breadth of ways in which universal, free-to-families, high-quality childcare would transform America should make it a calling of the banners. Nothing is going to change, not the big, bold, fundamental-structural-shift kind of change we need, without a lot more oomph behind a movement for making childcare a common good and an unconditional right.

Recall the story of punctuated equilibrium. Big shifts happens after long periods of stasis because of a critical mass of pressure. Milton Friedman, whatever you think of his economic ideas, hit on something when he wrote:

"There is enormous inertia — a tyranny of the status quo — in private and especially governmental arrangements. Only a crisis — actual or perceived — produces real change. When that crisis occurs, the actions that are taken depend on the ideas that are lying around. That, I believe, is our basic function: to develop alternatives to existing policies, to keep them alive and available until the politically impossible becomes politically inevitable."[187]

Well, we have an actual crisis on our hands. And if we don't respond with the verve that is called for, if we continue to accept quarter-measures and incremental gains, we will be having the same conversation in twenty years, except with far fewer parents around to speak up.

While I have been clear throughout the book that compromise is necessary, compromise can only occur within the boundaries of actually solving the overall crisis – the structural flaws in our childcare (non)-system. We can compromise on how Credits will be delivered or if there should be public centers for certain ages. We can compromise on how to apportion the Credit for stay-at-home parents with twin babies. What we *can't* compromise on is the fact that we require a multi-hundred-billion-dollar annual investment in our young children and young families, for they are flailing and we have a dim future without them. This is not audacious so much as it is a necessity, which in turn makes it attainable. As I hope I've shown, this minimum level of adequate funding is necessary to fix the system, yet no proposal on the table right now comes close. To compromise on this basic premise – childcare is a common good – is to haggle about the price of water when our neighbor's house is on fire, flames licking at our own roof.

Let's be clear: This is *not* intended to cast aspersions at the hard-working advocates who are striving day in and day out to improve childcare in America. They are doing their very best to make a broken system work for the families and children who need care right now. Moreover, through persistent effort and overcoming limited resources, these advocates have successfully shifted the conversation. Twenty years ago, childcare was in what one report termed a "silent" crisis; today it's a voiced priority of our policymakers.[188] My frustration is simply that we give up critical ground when we allow the issue to be framed as anything but a common good. While many proposed solutions are so timid as to be pebbles in the ocean – expanding dependent care flexible savings accounts, mildly raising the size of child-related tax credits, and so on – even the bolder ones don't go far enough.

Take the Childcare For Working Families Act, a major piece of legislation recently reintroduced by Senator Patty Murray (D-WA). This is a fabulous proposal in that it takes a big swing at the problem, and it puts a stake in the ground for important principles like pay parity between certain types of childcare teachers and their elementary school counterparts. The bill is centered on the idea that for families making under a certain amount of money, childcare costs should be capped at 7 percent of gross income, per the 'affordability' guidelines of the U.S. Department of Health and Human Services, with some of the poorest families paying nothing.

While this would be a significant improvement and I of course support the bill, there are a few foundational problems. First, a common good does not change its cost based on income. Roads don't become less free the wealthier you are, nor do only the poor get to stroll openly into a public park. Second, we don't cap common goods, they're just zero-cost to the public. You don't spend a max of 7 percent of your income on public schools or public sidewalks. Philosophically, accepting constraints like caps or income phase-outs shifts the conversation onto an entirely different ground. Childcare should be free because childcare is a common good. Full stop, period, and put the onus on opponents to make the case for why that's not true (and why they support free universal public education, if so).

Similarly, the biggest early childhood push around the nation right now is for the expansion of public pre-Kindergarten, which as a refresher offers free, formal slots to 4- and sometimes 3-year-olds. This is a classic 'school readiness' play, essentially marching the K-12 education system backward by adding earlier grades, as opposed to taking a family support starting-at-birth perspective. Again, it's infinity percent better than nothing. Moreover, pre-K expansion may offer a model for localities or states that want to use a mixed system of Credits for infants and toddlers and universal public centers for 3s and 4s (this is one of the 'Variations on a Theme' to come later).

However.

Pre-K expansion being set as a massive accomplishment – and politicians gaining plaudits for making any moves in that direction – once more puts the goalposts in the wrong place. Pre-K battles often take years to get resolved legislatively, and when they do, it's years more before they can be fully implemented. Take Washington, D.C., one of America's great pre-K success stories; currently, around 90 percent of D.C. 4-year-olds and 70 percent of 3-year-olds attend a pre-K program.[189] Focused work on what would become the "Pre-K for All DC" campaign began in 2003, and the campaign officially launched in 2006.[190] The legislation for universal pre-K passed in 2008, with the goal of being fully operational by 2014.[191] Given the trendlines we're seeing for families, it's not clear we have decades to spend wrangling over what amounts to at best two of the first five years of children's lives.

Given the need for a powerful alliance pushing urgently for birth-to-five structural change, why the silence from advocates in sectors that would advance their goals if we had free childcare? A kind interpretation is that the linkages aren't often explicitly made. I have read many, many articles and policy papers regarding childcare, and in almost none of them is abortion or environmentalism mentioned. The somewhat hairier reason is that because no one is pressuring other sectors to consider the bigger picture, they are steered down the path most closely at eye level.

Consider K-12 education again. This is the sector whose bottom line of student achievement is perhaps most directly impacted by the state of childcare. Yet, aside from statements of support, tangible K-12 support for childcare and family support policies – especially for infants and toddlers – is quite small and targeted almost solely at pre-K expansion[*]. Neither superintendents nor school boards, teachers unions nor 'education reformers,' are out there pushing hard to make childcare for the birth-to-five years free, high-quality, and widely accessible across all types of providers.

A closer look reveals that K-12 education stakeholders have perverse incentives not to push too hard around early childhood. Elliot Regenstein, an early education policy expert, has pointed out that most state accountability systems (standardized tests, etc.) start with 3rd grade when children are eight years old.[192] Given that the average tenure of a superintendent is somewhere between three and six years, and most school board members stand election every four, investing limited capacity in children who will likely never inform your performance review is a tricky proposition.[193]

It's particularly tricky because these leaders have other voices in their ears, speaking loudly about issues in the perceived here-and-now.

---

[*] The U.S. Department of Education has offered states Preschool Development Grants to the tune of $250 million (divided amongst a suite of winners) under both the Obama and Trump administrations. While useful, this has, as you can imagine, not changed the overall situation.

If there's a push for a big increase in public funding, teachers may reasonably want to see that going to their salaries or to lowering class sizes. A similar calculus undoubtedly exists for other sectors. While this isn't an either-or, it is shortsighted: fixing childcare, as we've seen, will lead to children arriving at school vastly more ready to learn and with families who have vastly more capacity to contribute; in the medium-term, the boost in economic productivity will lead to a sustainable increase in funding available for things like schools*. In the pyramidal hierarchy of children's policy needs, childcare forms the broad base.

The exception proves the rule here: recall that the one sub-sector that is starting to make moves towards supplying free, high-quality childcare is large private businesses. The pressure here is an economic one around retaining employees and avoiding lost productivity. Although, as the benefit is only offered at corporate HQ, the economic equation doesn't seem to apply to more fungible front-line workers, yet another reason why we can't just rely on market forces to fix this absent public investment.

Indeed, popular pressure on its own is rarely enough to catalyze major policy change; as we've seen, every expansion of the common good has been led in large part by the business community. The return-on-investment case is so strong that with the political shield of a massive movement of parents, CEOs should be able to assuage their boardrooms and shareholders that supporting free childcare is as good for the bottom line as it is for their public relations. Outside pressure from advocates and inside pressure from the donor class is a formula for getting lawmakers on board.

If Rick Santorum and George Miller can do it, so can your elected representatives.

---

* What's more, at least for education, there's an existential self-interest in curbing the falling birth rate: fewer students means fewer dollars and fewer teachers needed.

Chapter 10: Childcare Should Be Free for Families – and America Can Afford It

Running the Numbers

Our conversation now pivots from making the case for *why* childcare should be free for families to making the case for *how* childcare *could* be free for families. In short, how do we pay for this?

(Fair warning, this is going to get number heavy for just a minute.)

First, some back-of-the-envelope math to get a ballpark cost estimate:

There are about 20 million kids in the U.S. ages birth to five.[194] 20 million x $15,000 = $300 billion.

There are about 54 million kids in the U.S. ages five to eighteen. 54 million x $1,000 = $54 billion.

So, let's round to a nice even number and say that universal childcare would cost $350 billion a year*.

A couple more numbers to put that price tag in context. K-12 education spending per year – federal, state, and local – is over $650 billion per year (up from $250B just twenty-five years ago!).[195] Medicaid is $560 billion, Medicare $670 billion.[196]

All that to say, Child and Youth Development Credits aren't cheap, but they also aren't insane – they cost about half to two-thirds as much as other major social spending programs. Not a bad deal for an initiative that can simultaneously aid the social mobility of tens of millions of families, provide a major economic boost, and invigorate the healthy development of the entire next generation.

Two major elements also bring the $350 billion sticker price *way* down.

---

* In reality, of course, this number will get skewed by adjusting the amounts by cost-of-living, adding in administrative costs, etc. Adding in a child allowance would be an additional bump. That said, this isn't a wild guess, either – there's a reasonable probability the cost will fall in the $300-$400 billion/year range.

First, there's already a chunk of government spending aimed at young children – it's just enormously inefficient and ineffective. It can all be rolled up and used to pay for the new allocations. All of the various child-related tax credits currently on the books (the Child Tax Credit, Child and Dependent Care Tax Credit, Additional Child Credit, etc.) total around $60 billion*.[197] All federal childcare subsidies for low-income families† come out to around $21 billion. State spending on public pre-K totals $8 billion. Head Start is a little more than $7 billion. All told, that's a nearly $100 billion chunk – getting close to a third of the cost – off the top‡.

Second, while many social programs love to make the claim that they mostly pay for themselves, there's robust, empirical evidence that this one really does. That's because, in addition to the future benefits of high-quality early care and education (which Nobel Prize-winning economist James Heckman has shown to be enormous) and of reducing the number of children in poverty, there's the immediate benefit of getting many more people, mainly women, into the workforce. [198] This was certainly Quebec's experience – and the experience of a menagerie of nations as far-flung as Germany, Chile, and Israel – and we have similar evidence here at home.[199]

For instance, let's return for a moment to Washington, D.C. In 2009, universal pre-K for four- and three-year-olds in D.C. began to be phased in.[200] The years preceding 2009 saw a flat line of workforce participation among mothers with young children; it hovered around two-thirds§. A Center for American Progress (CAP) analysis found that with the launch of the pre-K program, this participation rate began a steady climb. In 2016 it was over 75 percent and still rising; the labor participation rate of mothers of those preschoolers now equals that of mothers with school-

---

* Some of these credits also apply to older children.
† Primarily through the Child Care and Development Fund and states transferring a piece of the Temporary Assistance for Needy Families program
‡ Presumably, if Head Start funds were converted into Credits, families could maintain their slots and just use the Credit at their Head Start site, since they're already not paying anything out of pocket. Programs that would *not* be rolled up include parenting supports like the Maternal, Infant, and Early Childhood Home Visiting (MIECHV) program and interventions aimed at children with special needs. Making childcare free does not eliminate all needs for young families.
§ The "labor participation rate" is defined as the percentage of people employed, or unemployed and actively seeking work

aged children. Notably, the rise in participation rate occurred at roughly the same rates among both lower-income and higher-income mothers.

FIGURE 3

Labor force participation of Washington, D.C., mothers with young children now matches that of Washington, D.C., mothers with school-age children
Difference-in-differences by age of child

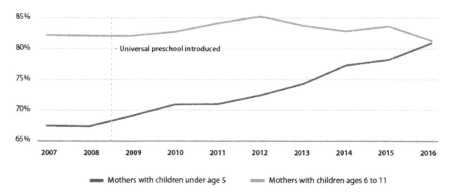

Mothers with children under age 5 — Mothers with children ages 6 to 11

Source: Author's analysis of Integrated Public Use Microdata Series American Community Survey data. See Steven Ruggles and others, "Integrated Public Use Microdata Series, U.S. Census Data for Social, Economic, and Health Research, American Community Survey: 5-year estimates" (Minneapolis: Minnesota Population Center at the University of Minnesota), available at https://usa.ipums.org/usa/ (last accessed August 2018).

In raw numbers, that's several thousand more D.C. women working. Several thousand more people adding productivity to local businesses, paying taxes, going out to lunch at neighborhood eateries, and, in the case of lower-income individuals, getting a chance to rise above the poverty line. These are immediate, tangible economic benefits.

The potential effect if applied nationwide? The CAP report notes that former Federal Reserve Chair Janet Yellen once "quoted a study that estimates that 'increasing the female participation rate to that of men would raise our gross domestic product by 5 percent.'"

The overall gap in the labor participation rate between men and women is about 10 percent.[201] Universal childcare — and this is a low-end estimate based on programs covering just some ages and/or not reaching all intended beneficiaries — seems to raise the female labor participation rate by between 5 percent and 10 percent.

One more bit of math:

The United States Gross Domestic Product = $19.39 trillion.[202]

Five percent of $19.39 trillion is $969.5 billion.

By the calculation of the researchers Yellen cited, Child and Youth

Development Credits would pay for themselves *nearly three times over* through only one of the Credits' many effects.

*   *   *

A Rising Tide Lifts All Boats

One of the other effects that would cause an immediate, non-theoretical return on investment is the revitalization of the childcare sector. It's tough to pin down exact numbers on how many people work in the sector because there's so much informal care, but the Center for the Study of Child Care Employment at UC-Berkeley pegs it at around approximately 2 million individuals.[203] That puts childcare workers in the top 15 of the highest-employment U.S. occupations; for context, there are slightly more than 3 million public school teachers, and around 1.5 million truckers.[204] Childcare is a big, important sector.

Given childcare teachers' exceedingly low wages (remember: an average of less than $23,000 a year) and common lack of benefits like health insurance, there are two major positive effects on the economy from increasing their base pay to, say, that of elementary school teachers. First, it will take a huge swath of people out of needing to access the public safety net – SNAP, Medicaid, the Earned Income Tax Credit, etc. While there's nothing wrong with needing temporary assistance, enabling a family to reach stability saves the government that outlay. The Berkeley research found that more than half of childcare workers were in households making so little money that they qualified for public assistance – and the majority of those teachers were working full-time! Bringing the number of childcare teachers accessing public assistance in line with that of elementary teachers would reduce the public assistance rolls by 600,000 or more. That would save the government billions.

Second, this proposal would also significantly increase the amount of purchases these two million-plus families could make, as well as the income and sales tax they would pay. And, in a virtuous cycle, because they too would have access to the Child and Youth Development Credits for their own children, they would have a pathway to continued social mobility (it's worth noting again that this would also be a win for equity, as the childcare workforce is almost entirely female and disproportionately made up of people of color).

Additionally, given the tremendous unfilled demand, the likely opening of tens of thousands of childcare providers offering a living wage would provide new employment opportunities. This would reduce unemployment and underemployment while increasing government coffers via payroll taxes, business licensing fees, and so on. Similarly, because families using nannies would need to note that in order to use the credit, the staggeringly high rate of non-payment of 'nanny taxes' would plummet*. One economist estimates that the country could recoup between $3.3 and $5.7 billion annually if everyone paid the nanny taxes they're supposed to.[205]

*   *   *

The other philosophical question here is, why spend $350 billion annually on childcare and not something else? Depending on your political persuasion, one might make the case that we should use that on investing in green energy or providing a tax break for small businesses or public transportation or giving out a universal basic income. Any spending program comes with opportunity costs — because you're spending it on X, you're not spending it on Y.

Childcare stands out as a unique candidate for public investment because of its status as a should-be common good. Investing in spurring small business growth may well be good policy, but it doesn't hold the same societal imperative. The list of true common goods is relatively small: national defense, infrastructure (roads, sewers), safety (fire/police), education (schools), public spaces (parks, sidewalks), that's about it. Even things like housing and food are broadly considered private, not common, goods. Yet as I've laid out, childcare almost inarguably belongs on the common good list. Much like public education, it undergirds the entire American Dream. It allows children and their parents the opportunity to achieve their self-defined aspirations while enriching the community and country and safeguarding the future from a birth rate standpoint. It also frees up

---

* Nannies are, legally speaking, household workers, and employing families are required to pay payroll taxes, etc. The rate of compliance is as low at 5 percent. You may recall this has gotten some government nominees in trouble from time to time.

families' bandwidth to tackle social issues that are higher up the hierarchy of needs (more on this in a later chapter). Altogether, that's about as common a good as you'll find.

Still, that being said, let's be clear: The odds of the federal government enacting this program on its own are perhaps slim, though they are certainly best positioned to come up with the funding. It's likely going to fall first to states or cities.

*   *   *

First Through the Gate

What we need for a proof point is a small state, ideally left-leaning (it just smooths the path for spending more money and helping families), with a decent wealth base.

Enter Rhode Island.

Actually, what we need is a state that has both rural areas and at least one good-sized city, ideally right-leaning (it just smooths the path for giving parents choice and helping businesses), with a rapidly rising population of young families.

Let's go back to Idaho.

I generalize and joke, of course, but it's to make a point. At some point, a governor or mayor is going to realize that the childcare crisis is rotting the foundation of his or her constituency, and they're going to act. States have traditionally been the laboratories for social change, ranging from Wyoming giving women the vote way back in 1890 to Massachusetts' early adoption of gay marriage to Colorado and Washington State's adoption of legalized marijuana. It's been a similar story in the birth-to-5 world: Free, broadly accessible pre-K in places like New Jersey and Tulsa, Oklahoma laid the groundwork for the nationwide expansion we're seeing today[*].

I cite Rhode Island and Idaho because the best candidate states for piloting Child Development Credits are likely those that are on the bottom half of the population rankings. Rhode Island only has 55,000

---

[*] It's worth noting that on issues like gay marriage and pre-K, it was sometimes the legislature and sometimes the courts that were behind the change. Perhaps there's a state where the case could be made that treating 0-to-5 as a publicly-funded right is required by constitutional interpretation?

kids aged birth-to-five, Wyoming 37,000. My home state of Virginia has over 500,000. That order of magnitude matters when in the proof-of-concept stage.

States where there's a major gap in the female-to-male labor participation rates also stand out as strong options, given the immediate cost defrayment of women entering the workforce. Idaho, for instance, has a nearly 17 percent gender gap in labor participation among men and women ages 25-34 (years where parents are very likely to have young children).[206] In Delaware, it's 13 percent. These states have more to gain from a purely economic standpoint than, say, another small population state like Vermont, where the gender labor gap is 'only' 7 percent.

Whatever state or city is first through the gate is going to reap tremendous benefits. Imagine the appeal of a state or city that is hemorrhaging population, like a West Virginia or a Cleveland (OH), suddenly being able to brand themselves as the friendliest place in America for families. Imagine the infusion of talent. Imagine the pitch to businesses that suddenly will have a big ol' carrot to hang in front of workers and who will know they have a more stable and satisfied workforce at hand. The first jurisdiction to put free childcare into place is going to be like the first 49ers to Sutter's Mill.

* * *

When It's Important, We Find the Money

While I hope I've made the case in this chapter that universal, free-to-families childcare is surprisingly affordable, I'm not going to suggest a specific financing scheme*. States and localities are too individual to make any kind of blanket statement. Presumably, it will require a mixture of reallocation of existing dollars and generation of new tax revenue.

I will, however, note that these are not flights of fancy. For example,

---

* Nor am I going to suggest a specific qualification scheme that dissuades people from gaming the system, but I'll note that there are models out there – Alaska's Permanent Fund gives out an annual stipend to residents based on certain enforceable requirements,

the Congressional Budget Office (CBO) puts out an annual list of tax maneuvers that would either save or cost the government money. One of the options they noted in their 2018 edition is what's known as a financial transaction tax. A financial transaction tax is simply a tax on the sale or purchase of high finance products – stocks, bonds, and the such. It doesn't touch everyday transactions like check deposits or ATM withdrawals. The CBO estimates that levying a mere 0.1 percent tax on high finance would bring in a reliable $100 billion year after year.[207] Other analyses on the financial transaction tax have shown that the rich pick up most of the tab since the vast majority of Americans have little to no direct engagement with the stock market.

Alternatively, consider the "tax gap," which is the amount of taxes that are either underreported or not reported at all to the IRS. Because we don't adequately fund the IRS, it's quite easy to get away with not fully paying one's tax liability, particularly for corporations and wealthier individuals (the easiest folks for the IRS to catch are ordinary workers, because of the employer's automatic W-2 and 1099 submissions; it's when you have business income and stocks and the such that you can start playing games with little fear of being caught). If all Americans paid what they actually owed in taxes – and, again, it's not the Walmart employee or Walgreens pharmacy tech who's bilking the government – the IRS estimates we'd have another $400 billion a year to play with, enough to pay for free childcare in one move.[208]

These are just two illustrations among many to make a simple point: There are real sources of untapped revenue if we build up enough political steam to make bold choices.

It'll be up to the staff of that brave president or governor or mayor to figure out what exactly the revenue matrix looks like. All I'll offer here is that everything should be on the table. The economic benefits make it much more palatable to consider asking business to chip in via corporate taxes, to ask the wealthy to pay a fairer share via capital gains or wealth taxes, or to consider raising local income or sales taxes. Perhaps this is an area ripe for directing cannabis tax revenues as marijuana legalization continues to spread across the nation.

In the end, it's money, but it's not *that* much money. For a mid-sized city, the proposition can be posed as raising the budget from $700,000,000 to $800,000,000 in exchange for slicing the poverty rate by double-digits, providing rocket fuel for educational and economic outcomes, stabilizing/attracting young families, and contributing to the thriving of the entire community. It's a steal at ten times the price.

When it's important, we find the money. This is important.

Childcare should be free – and we can afford it.

Chapter 11: The Future of Families

Down, Down, Down

It's not hyperbole to suggest that we're facing a crossroads that will define the future of American families. In this chapter, we're going to pull up and consider just how big the stakes are, and just how broad our response must be.

If we do not do something about the raging childcare crisis, the trend lines we've seen emerge are only going to get worse. This means more and more closures among formal childcare providers and childcare desertification spreading to every corner of the nation. With few options – and with Baby Boomers rapidly aging towards the point where grandparents cannot serve as caregivers (indeed, more often requiring caregivers themselves, which is a whole different book) – more and more parents will be forced into the gray market of unregulated care. Yet even this gray market won't be able to bear the weight of the demand, causing a forced exodus of parents (mostly mothers) out of the workforce to provide care. Except, as we've seen, for the overwhelming majority of the bottom-income 90 percent – and 100 percent of single parents – families can't afford to lose an earner.

What are the consequences? On an individual level, people are going to drastically reduce the number of children they are having, or stop having children altogether. Most couples will lose the right of choosing their family size, just as some of the families we've met in this book have, and large families will become a privilege only owned by the truly rich.

This is not a vision of some dystopian future, it's already happening.

The rich are the only ones having *more* babies than before, which gives away the game as to why everyone else is having less. Reversing the conventional wisdom that it's the poor who have the most kids, the greatest relative share of three-child households actually now lies with families making over $500,000 a year.[209] One set of researchers, Moshe

Hazan and Hosni Zoabi, dubbed this phenomenon the "U-shaped fertility" curve (in other words, the very poor and very rich are having the most children).[210] Another way of looking at this is that the most highly-educated mothers — a proxy for affluence — are suddenly defying historical patterns. Traditionally, this group has had the lowest fertility rates, but when you break down contemporary data by educational attainment, they're now the group with the fastest-growing family sizes.[211]

The reason is obvious: the rich are the only ones who can *afford* to have these big nests. Hazan and Zoabi concluded that among the affluent, "highly educated women substitute a significant part of their own [provision of parental childcare] with [outside] childcare. This enables them to have more children and work longer hours." There's even an uncomfortable status symbol component at play for some: a 2014 *New York Times* article on the growth of three-child families among the wealthy set in New York City quoted one father as saying, "At some level, the third child is a proxy for having enough wealth to have a very comfortable life."[212]

For the children that are born to the non-affluent, especially those in families below the ALICE or poverty lines, they are increasingly likely to grow up in high-stress households. As we've seen, if risk factors for negative life outcomes spoke a language, it would be the language of stress. This language, made up of an alphabet of hormones like cortisol and adrenaline, has cascading effects on both the body and the environment in which the body exists. As the eminent neuroscientist Robert Sapolsky puts it in his tour-de-force book, *Behave: The Biology of Humans at our Best and Worst:*

"Sustained stress has numerous adverse effects. The amygdala becomes overactive and more coupled to pathways of habitual behavior; it is easier to learn fear and harder to unlearn it. We process emotionally salient information more rapidly and automatically, but with less accuracy. Frontal function – working memory, impulse control, executive decision making, risk assessment, and task shifting – is impaired, and the frontal cortex has less control over the amygdala. And we become less empathic and prosocial."[213]

Is it any wonder that chronic familial stress is correlated with significantly higher rates of divorce, domestic violence, abuse, neglect, and less attentive parenting? There's also a nasty cycle at play here: parents have to work longer hours to pay for care – or to make up for lost income of a partner exiting the workforce to provide care – which leads to being tired, stressed out, and having less time with their children.

To extend the metaphor perhaps near its breaking point, stress, when inscribed over and over again like Bart Simpson at the blackboard, starts to rewrite entire stories. There is evidence that high levels of stress can literally be passed down from generation to generation. Most directly, pregnant women under chronic or acute stress tend to have babies with more overactive stress responses – the environment in the womb dictates a great deal of fetal development, and when mom's body is flooded with stress hormones, it's a signal to the baby to prepare itself for a scary world. A striking example of this came from a study which found altered stress response systems in the babies of pregnant women who were in New York City on 9/11/01.[214]

Stress can even alter our very gene expression via epigenetics (while life experiences can't change DNA, it turns out they can change the package that carries the DNA). This is certainly true in rats – take a non-stressed female rat, put it with a stressed-out mom that neglects it, and the previously serene rat's pups are more likely to have an overactive stress response[*][215] – and there is growing confirmation it's true in humans as well.[216] While I hope I've proven throughout this text that neither genetics nor negative life experiences are destiny, it's fair to say that time may in fact not heal all wounds.

Beyond the myriad stress consequences, growing up in a financially burdened household also means less access to opportunity. That includes everything from extracurricular activities to the ability to take unpaid or low-paying internships that could have an outsized impact on career interests and prospects[†]. It's a great way for our society to miss out on the next great artist, inventor, or entrepreneur. As a quote attributed to Leila Janah goes, "talent is distributed equally, opportunity is not."

Indeed, there is more at stake here than even the well-being of our

---

[*] Though if you take *those* frazzled pups and puts them with a nurturing mother, the epigenome – and their stress response – stabilizes back to normal. Early adverse experiences are not destiny, particularly if we can tamp down the toxic stress as soon as possible.

[†] Memo to organizations: pay your interns a living wage.

children and our families – the future of families is inextricably tied to the future of communities, the nation, and ultimately the world. Right now, the lack of free, available, high-quality childcare is threatening that future.

*   *   *

We Need the Voices of Parents and Families

Most of the families we've met in this book are bringing in a solid income, which is why their struggles create such a stunning picture of the future of families. If two-earner, college-educated couples near the top of the middle class are barely able to make ends meet due to childcare costs, it suggests just how dire the situation is at all the rungs below*. Stress, beyond all of its other ills, has one other insidious effect: it causes the mind to 'tunnel,' to focus on immediate short-term needs.[217] This tunneling can literally cause everything else to be out of sight and out of mind; consider when you're super-stressed because you're running late for work or in the midst of a big fight with a partner and bump into a telephone pole or bystander you could have sworn wasn't there a second ago. Psychologist Eldar Shafir and behavioral economist Sendhil Mullainathan have run studies showing that as far as your mind was concerned, it (or he/she) wasn't. While tunneling isn't ideal in the day-to-day, it's especially problematic when there are a lot of big long-term needs out there which need the leadership of families.

Abraham Maslow famously created his "hierarchy of needs" for individuals: our attention is first demanded by physical needs like food and safety, and as those are taken care of, we turn to more high-minded pursuits like needing love and self-actualization. It seems to me that families have a similar hierarchy – financial stability comes before civic engagement. As Ruth Watt put it to me, reflecting on her family's lack of funds to pay for temporary care: "Going to the state capitol to visit state legislators with a 6-year-old, 4-year-old, 2-year-old and newborn in tow sounds like a really awesome way to make sure I am unable to carry

---

* In *Squeezed*, Alissa Quart uses the phrase "middle precariat" to describe this new reality for the previously comfortable middle class – "precariat" being a portmanteau of "precarious" and "proletariat" first coined by sociologist Guy Standing.

on a meaningful conversation."

Indeed, a large body of literature has generally found an inverse correlation between income and civic participation.[218] This is not because people who are less affluent care less about their communities, but because of the hopefully obvious barriers presented by being financially strapped. It's hard to get to a 3:00 p.m. City Council budget hearing downtown when you work multiple shift jobs in the suburbs or can't afford a babysitter, and it's hard to even to find the mental bandwidth to think about the city budget. More time spent working, more time spent stressing, less time spent engaging in current affairs[*].

Yet parent voices are badly needed. Parents – particularly parents of young children – are, on the whole, more likely to take a long view on issues because they know the consequences will apply to their kids. Parental self-interest is inherently future-oriented in a different way than the self-interest of non-parents (although these are just broad predilections: you can easily find *plenty* of selfish parents and *plenty* of communally-minded singletons)[†]. Fred Rogers put it this way: "Parents are like shuttles on a loom. They join the threads of the past with threads of the future and leave their own bright patterns as they go."

Indeed, despite the challenges, it's more often than not a parent who is standing before their city councilor complaining about a lack of safe sidewalks on the route to school, or cars speeding down the side street where their children play. The sidewalks and speed bumps that result from this advocacy benefit everyone in the neighborhood, but their genesis is families. Moreover, children are a kind of 'universal donor' of politics: they make just about any message more powerful, and it's awfully hard to argue against them. The presence of children also seems to have an overall salubrious effect. One research brief noted that looking across 22 developed nations, "countries with cheaper out-of-pocket costs for childcare had happier nonparents as well as parents,

[*] There are also social and cultural barriers at play. Historian Sonya Michel quotes political theorist Carole Pateman's observation that because they are (unfairly) seen as not pulling their economic weight, "Citizens thrown into poverty lack ... the means to be recognized by fellow citizens as of equal worth to themselves, a recognition basic to democracy," and notes this phenomenon has often played out when it comes to mothers.
[†] Some of this is biologically coded; to *vastly* oversimply, it's fair to say that parents are on some level driven to see their genes passed on via their children.

perhaps because everyone benefits when children are well -socialized and their cognitive development is prioritized in early childhood."[219]

In sum, families with children are at the heart of what a recent National Academies of Medicine paper called a community's sense of "collective efficacy." Collective efficacy is a measure of social health answering the question "can individuals work together to accomplish their goals?"[220] The authors note that "children are embedded in families, who are, in turn, embedded in neighborhoods and communities," and therefore "strengthened family and community contexts increase the capacity for community cohesiveness, thus activating a sense of meaning and purpose."

Meanwhile, there are issues requiring collective efficacy that dwarf safe streets, like a rapidly warming planet. It is disheartening, to say the very least, to consider what kind of world my daughters and potential grandchildren will be experiencing as the 21st century unfolds. Here, again, parents should be on the front lines, knowing that even if we may not personally see entire cities and coastlines disappear, those small, innocent eyes looking up at us almost certainly will. There are also directly negative impacts on our young children: We know that climate change is causing the resurgence of certain types of diseases, and research suggests that worldwide, nearly *90 percent* of the disease burden (reduced life expectancy, increased disability rate, etc.) attributable to climate change will fall on children under the age of five.[221]

Interestingly though, research from British communications expert George Marshall has found that on average, people with children show *less* concern about climate change than those without children.[222] Why? Partially it's due to human psychological bias – we're inclined to justify our decision to bring children into an uncertain world, not embrace the danger we've exposed them to – and largely because parents are simply overwhelmed*. In the words of one expert, Marshall "found that, in fact, parents often appeared less concerned because they were so fixated on the day-to-day challenges of raising a family."[223] I can certainly relate. Trying to make our family budget lines match up can reliably drain me of energy to, say, protest a natural gas pipeline. It's mental tunneling,

---

* It's worth noting that this research is a few years old, while evidence of global warming's impacts have been rapidly making an appearance. It's possible this would no long hold true.

writ global.

We're losing the voices of families at the worst possible historical moment, and as fertility rates continue to drop, the threat to pro-family policies will only increase. Jonathan Last, author of the book *What To Expect When No One's Expecting*, put it this way in a 2013 Wall Street Journal op-ed:

"Low-fertility societies don't innovate because their incentives for consumption tilt overwhelmingly toward health care. They don't invest aggressively because, with the average age skewing higher, capital shifts to preserving and extending life and then begins drawing down. They cannot sustain social-security programs because they don't have enough workers to pay for the retirees. They cannot project power because they lack the money to pay for defense and the military-age manpower to serve in their armed forces."[224]

Nor, I might add to the list, can low-fertility societies fully reckon with the economic transformations necessary to mitigate our climate crisis. There are also serious long-term political implications here: less kids means an electorate that skews older – and, on the whole, elderly voters and young voters have starkly different preferences and perspectives[*]. An imbalanced electorate is dangerously unlikely to find the right mix of current- and future-facing policies. In other words, the time for change is now, before it's too late.

* * *

Family Support Is More Than Just Childcare

While free, high-quality childcare is the bedrock of a family-friendly society, it's not the only needed policy. Ideally, we would have an arc of policies that, threading seamlessly like connective tissue, bolsters families from pregnancy through childhood. An example of this approach has been offered by Matt Bruenig, the People's Policy Project analyst. In early 2019, Bruenig released a set of family support proposals

---

[*] As one example, in the United Kingdom's 2016's "Brexit" vote, 60% of voters over 65 voted to leave the European Union, while 73% of voters aged 18-24 voted to remain.

he collectively termed the Family Fun Pack.[225]

The Pack, which includes a version of free childcare, is premised on a broader analysis of why families struggle so much in our current economy. Bruenig makes a two-pronged argument. First is what he calls the "mere addition" problem: "Adding children to a family unit increases the number of resources and time needed by the unit, but our current economic system does nothing to address this need. Similar workers receive the same wages and time off even though some have to pay for diapers and childcare while others do not … since children increase the amount of resources families need to maintain their standard of living, a society that fails to match that need with public benefits will generally wind up with high levels of interfamily inequality and high levels of child and child-adjacent poverty."

The second problem Bruenig calls out was referenced in this book's introduction. The "lifecycle income problem" is the basic fact that we tend to have children way before hitting our prime earning years. Bruenig concludes that "put simply, the distribution of income in a capitalist economy is at odds with the rhythm of human life and especially the rhythm of family life. Child-bearing comes too early to amass savings. Income arrives too late to finance contemporaneous child-related expenditures. Even the patterning of income during parenthood itself is nonsensical: parents of older children have higher incomes than parents of younger children despite the fact that older children do not require [full-time] childcare and even though the younger years are the most crucial for child development."

To respond to these structural problems, the Family Fun Pack offers a series of solutions, ranging from small to large in their scope. They also range from relatively neutral to political hot potatoes (such as a proposal for free health care – essentially Medicare-for-All – for all individuals under the age of 26). While I don't endorse every detail of Bruenig's proposals, they show how Child and Youth Development Credits can and should fit into an integrated suite of supports across childhood. As we've seen, children do not develop in a vacuum; every aspect of family wellness creates the developmental environment, so isolating only one aspect, or one age, or one set of hours of the day, is an inherently flawed strategy. In particular, three proposals not directly related to childcare warrant lifting up:

- **"Baby Boxes" for every family**: Baby Boxes are a Northern European tradition that is starting to catch on elsewhere – including the U.S. – whereby expectant families get a sturdy box and mattress that can act as a safe sleeping space for baby's first few months, as well as a starter kit of baby essentials like diapers and wipes. This is a simple, low-cost way to reduce infant mortality and let parents start their journey without a scarcity mindset.

- **Paid parental leave** (Bruenig proposes 36 weeks), splittable among the primary parents/guardians. There have been many words written about the indignity of lack of decent U.S. parental leave policies, so it's not worth belaboring the point – though it is worth writing twice in this book that one-in-four American women are back at work within *two weeks* of giving birth! While the Credit system can serve as a stand-in for parental leave, real paid leave policies are better both functionally and in what they communicate about the value we place on families, and mothers in particular.

- **An unrestricted Child Allowance** (Bruenig proposes $300 per month per child). While childcare costs are what hits families like a financial avalanche, there are other significant costs associated with raising children. As noted earlier, a child allowance is a critical companion to the Credits. This benefit, unlike the Credits, should likely be means-tested (phasing out for higher-income families). Child allowances, sometimes called 'child benefits', are common in other countries, and study after study finds that the money does, in fact, go to paying for child-rearing expenses or other necessities like food.[226] There's little more harrowing than the idea of not having the cash on hand to provide your baby with basic needs like diapers or formula, yet there's a reason baby formula is one of the most stolen items.[227] There's also a reason some childcare providers have a heart-wrenching term – "Monday-morning rash" – for the rash babies get from being in a soiled diaper too long over the weekend because their parents have to stretch a limited supply.[228]

There are certainly other proposals not included in the Family Fun Pack worth considering. One important intersection of health and child development is ensuring all women have access to high-quality, culturally comfortable prenatal and postnatal care. Policy solutions here could include things like making doulas and other maternal support professionals fully coverable by insurance and Medicaid at solid reimbursement rates. I'm also partial to "Baby Bonds," which seek to address racial and income inequality by investing in children's long-term wealth through giving every baby a savings account into which the government deposits some sum of money depending on family income level[*].[229]

The broader point, though, is that we need to have a serious national conversation about the future of families. That future is currently bleak, but we have tools and policy proposals at our disposal to turn the plane out of its nosedive. After all, on an elemental level, the future of families is the future of America.

Childcare should be free to families, yes. But in the final analysis, even that truth is a means to a bigger, brighter end: All children and families should have the opportunity to thrive.

---

[*] The money becomes accessible when the baby turns 18; some proposals restrict usage of the money to asset-building actions like attending college, buying a home, starting a business, etc.

CHAPTER 12: Variations on a Theme

While I've tried to make a case for why Child Development Credits may have the most promise as a solution to the American childcare crisis, I fully acknowledge there are other paths up the mountain of universal, free-to-families, high-quality care. I also think, again, it's critical that the conversation around these ideas doesn't become bogged down in the pros and cons of a specific proposal, but rather the core question: *Do we accept the premise that childcare should be a common good?* Therefore, I want to sketch out a few alternatives before wrapping up.

To go even a step further, if I were to critique my own proposal for the Credits system, I would home in on two main areas. First, it's possible that disparate results would arise among different income brackets. As mentioned in Section I, there's a chance poorer parents may end up utilizing the cash opt-out to meet their family's survival needs, almost using it as a child allowance and leaving less of the Credit remaining for acquiring high-quality care. More affluent parents, meanwhile, would have the full Credit at their disposal. Second, I may be overly optimistic about the power of the marketplace and in assuming that parents will have the information they need to ferret out bad actors. While there are tradeoffs, the major value of public centers is that they have a reliable minimum quality threshold and don't have any profit motive.

Ideally, states and cities will adopt their own unique variations of universal childcare (with federal support), and we'll be able to see in real time what actually happens. As I said way back in the Note on Proposals, that's exactly how it should work.

Without further ado, here are the variations:

A Mixed System For Different Ages

I've hinted at this one throughout the book. Though I ultimately find a discordance in the school readiness-focused philosophy of early childhood, there's a perfectly reasonable case to be made that three- and four-year-olds are able to participate in more discrete pre-academic activities than infants and young toddlers. Pre-K programs are still fundamentally play-based, but there's definitely an eye towards what kids will need to be able to do come Kindergarten – writing their names, knowing the alphabet, and so on. We also have much more of an infrastructure in place for these pre-K programs via Head Start and state's public pre-K systems, as well as robust models from other countries.

As a result, an alternative could be accepting an artificial line drawn at a child's third birthday. Birth to three, and their care is provided via the Credits; three to five, it's universal public pre-K. One important element of this alternative would be upping the per-child expenditures for public pre-K to the $15,000 base level. Keeping the per-child allocations as low as they are now (usually between $5,000-$10,000) would be providing access without ensuring quality, for instance keeping teachers at a relatively low pay level.

A Wholly Public System

Moving away from a mixed model to one extreme, there could be a universal public childcare system where all children birth-to-five are given the option to attend public centers. This might be termed the "Quebec option." As detailed in the book, the biggest challenge with the Quebec option is that neither Quebec nor any other jurisdiction has figured out how to provide enough public slots[*] – they all end up utilizing community-based and/or private providers, which creates all sorts of complex financing and oversight issues. That said, with enough public investment, the infrastructure barrier could be hurdled. Because it would all be regulated group care, the average per-child cost in a wholly public system would likely need to be closer to $25,000 than $15,000, which does raise the price tag. The advantage here, as noted above, is that public systems tend to be more democratically accountable and it's far easier to pull levers that ensure quality. If there's no (or only a small) cash opt-out, a public system skirts the potential issue of poor parents facing a no-win choice, as it would strongly incentivize using the public centers just like our current K-12 system strongly incentivizes

---

[*] Few jurisdictions have even been able to crack this nut when it comes to providing pre-K for four-year-olds, much less across five years' worth of age bands.

using public schools over homeschooling.

A Wholly Voucherized System

On the other extreme is the "Libertarian option," whereby you just hand the Credit to a family and get out of the way. No accreditation required, no quality rating and improvement system required – essentially, no guardrails. This is a pure free-market approach which I think history tells us is likely to lead to not-insignificant levels of abuse and inequity. It's an option that is, as you might guess, not my cup of tea. There is, however, a certain elegance in its simplicity, and it certainly minimizes administrative costs.

Different Credit Amounts Depending on Age, Setting, and Quality Level

As we've discussed, in group settings, infant care is quite a bit more expensive than care for a four-year-old because of the lower adult-to-child ratios required. For instance, a Center for American Progress study estimates that the true average cost of high-quality center care[*] for infants is about $25,000, versus $20,000 for toddlers and $15,000 for pre-K aged (three- and four-year-old) children.[230] While some of the cost differentials come out in the wash – because you can hold more pre-K kids per classroom, it can offset the smaller number of more expensive infants – it's still a significant issue, and a major reason why infant and toddler care is currently so scarce. It might make a lot of sense to assign more dollars to a Credit for infants and have it descend as children get older. This does raise some questions for FFN and parental care, however, because if you're only caring for one kid, it's not necessarily more expensive between an infant and three-year-old. Perhaps the best solution is that group-care settings (i.e., centers and home-based providers) that have more than a minimum number of children get a Credit supplement to offset the age cost differential.

Similarly, there's a significant body of research demonstrating that it costs more money to maintain a high-quality program than a

---

[*] The definition of high-quality CAP used in this study includes things like childcare teachers having salary parity with kindergarten teachers, low child-to-teacher ratios, paid planning time for teachers, etc.

mediocre one.[231] This makes intuitive sense: If you're doing things like hiring substitute teachers so your regular teachers can go to a professional development training, that's going to cost more. As a result, a majority of states currently use a form of "tiered reimbursement" for programs that get our meager public subsidy dollars: simply put, if you're higher-rated on the state's Quality Rating and Improvement System (say, a 4-star program), you get more per child than if you're lower-rated. While the $15,000 Credits should enable all providers to have the means to provide a strong program, differences in quality will still exist. Providing an additional supplement for higher-rated formal and informal programs could further incentivize and sustain quality.

Modified Credit Amounts Depending on Child Needs

There is an increasingly well-known distinction between "equality" and "equity" (some may prefer to use "fairness" as a synonym for equity). Equality means everyone gets the same thing, equity means everyone gets what they need. You may be familiar with the picture of people of different heights standing behind a fence trying to watch a baseball game; equality is they each get the same sized box to stand on, equity is they each get enough boxes to let them see over the fence:

Source: Interaction Institute for Social Change | Artist: Angus Maguire

An equity case for Child Development Credits – and one I'd support – would suggest that some children will need more than the base amount.

In particular, children with special needs may need a Credit boost, as might children from low-income backgrounds, children in foster care, and/or children for whom English is not their first language. These are traditionally the subgroups that receive extra funding in state K-12 education funding formulas for exactly the same reason – it enables them to get access to the equitable opportunities. For very young children, this might look like being able to access care with a lower adult-to-child ratio (more expensive), care with trained bilingual teachers (more expensive), or care at a therapeutic provider expert in helping children who have experienced trauma (more expensive).

This supplemental Credit could either be tacked on to the registration form or in many cases automatically applied by cross-referencing government systems – for instance, when a young child enters the care of Child Protective Services. It's relatively easy to establish eligibility for a supplement: children with special needs already have access to some services via Part B and Part C of the federal Individuals with Disabilities Education Act (IDEA), tax returns prove income, etc. The key, as always, is ensuring that all kids and families have access to the childcare they need.

CONCLUSION: Punctuating the Equilibrium

Learning that you are going to have a child should be one of the most joyous experiences in life. For far too many American families, that first burst of enthusiasm is quickly sullied by anxiety about childcare. A friend once wryly told me that the first person who knew she was pregnant was her partner, and the second was a center director. Family life in the wealthiest country on Earth should not be like this.

As we have seen, there are few contemporary issues more cross-cutting than the childcare crisis. It impacts families across geographic, economic, and ideological lines. It poses a threat to the stability of individual families as well as communities, cities, states, and ultimately, the nation and the world. Moreover, the childcare crisis is a chasm that threatens to swallow up the developmental trajectories of millions of American children while winnowing the very size of future generations.

It comes back to this truism: childcare is a common good and therefore requires robust public investment. Imagine for a moment that public K-12 education in America was suddenly no longer free, no longer a right. Parents would need to come up with fees – an average of about $11,000 per child – or else figure out alternative arrangements.

The entire system would break down overnight. Panicked parents rearranging their entire budgets and zeroing out their savings; others frantically calling grandparents and aunts and cousins to find someone to take the kids; a 'gray market' of cheap, low-quality options popping up; missed days of work, missed nights of sleep as mothers and fathers stare at the ceiling gripped by unyielding stress.

This is the situation we have allowed to arise for the early childhood years.

If anything, modern brain science tells us that if you were going to direct public investment to one age range, it would be early childhood. Every future life outcome links back to healthy development in the first years of life and every family outcome of the current generation links back to the ability to secure affordable, high-quality care.

The ground is rumbling, the volcano steaming as the childcare crisis deepens. What we can't do, however, is nothing. We cannot wait and hope that the crisis gets so very bad that our leaders eventually have no choice but to act. It will be too late by then; in truth, the hour grows late already, given that any solution will take years to implement.

So, here's the call to action: We need to start being the pressure. We need to pressure our elected and appointed leaders at the local, state, and federal levels. Not only our city councilors and mayors and legislators and governors but school board members and board of health members, too. We need to pressure our superintendents and principals, our local Chambers of Commerce, our university and college presidents. We need to get in front of pastors and rabbis and imams and tell them the faith community's voice is needed – after all, the story of nearly every religion is on some level a story about family and children. And we need to tap our networks of friends and relatives, even those who don't have young children, and tell them that our families are hanging off the edge of a cliff and it's going to take a collective effort to pull them back onto solid ground.

The messages will need to be tailored – for better or worse, humans respond to what they perceive as their self-interest. But a system of free-to-families, high-quality care that enables stable families and strong children is so fundamental to the social and economic underpinnings of our nation that it can speak to the self-interest of just about anyone.

America's current childcare (non-)system is breaking down. It has broken down already for most people, in fact, and the crisis is spreading. The good news is that we can fix it. In fact, I suspect we will, and we'll look back in the next century and marvel that anyone ever thought the birth-to-five years were a purely private problem where families should be required to come up with the money to supply high-quality care. That change, though, is not a given. It's going to take all of us to punctuate the equilibrium, to turn the politically impossible into the politically inevitable.

It all starts with that simple, bold-yet-commonsense idea:

Childcare should be free for families.

When we get there, we'll break through to a brighter future. One where all children have the opportunity to develop healthily and fulfill their self-defined potential, where parents can choose the number of kids and work situations they want, where families have both the quantity and quality of time needed to thrive and in turn radiate virtue throughout their communities. In short, instead of crawling behind, families will be leading the way.

Acknowledgements

If it takes a village to raise a child, then it certainly takes a village to write a book about childcare. I am indebted to many people. First of all, the families who were willing to bravely and vulnerably share their stories so readers could get their arms around the breadth of the crisis (go check out the Tang's Rooster & Owl next time you're in D.C., by the way – the *Washington Post*'s food critic Tom Sietsema called it D.C.'s "most exciting restaurant debut" of 2019). Thoughtful, essential feedback was provided by a set of early readers, Anthony LaMesa, Alyson Williams, and Laura Kane. Special shout-outs to Jason Amirhadji and Jarrod Shappell for both their encouragement and *long* back-and-forths as disparate ideas were forming themselves into the coherent framework for a book.

I wouldn't have made the career shift into early childhood without Kathy Glazer and the entire Virginia Early Childhood Foundation team (Marilyn Rice is the reason my children attend a high-quality center; here's to the entire hard-working staff at VCUHS Northside!), and I wouldn't be able to continue working towards systems change without Kelly Chopus and the entire Robins crew. On the writing front, I'm grateful to Alissa Quart and David Wallis of the Economic Hardship Reporting Project, and Janet Manley at Romper, for helping me get an initial excerpt of the book out into the world, and to Reagan Rothe and Black Rose Writing for bringing out the rest of it.

On a more personal level, I want to thank the community of friends and family that have surrounded us since Melissa's brain cancer diagnosis. To even have the bandwidth to research and write a book amid such a chaotic time is a testament to the many, many hands holding us up. There isn't a mathematical quantity capable of expressing my gratitude.

Finally, my adoration and appreciation for Melissa. In addition to your brilliant thought partnership and life partnership, your resilience, strength, candor, creativity, and capacity for love are a truly unique combination. Your support means the world to me, and the world is a better place for having your light in it.

Endnotes

1. Cain Miller, C. "Americans Are Having Fewer Babies. They Told Us Why." The New York Times, July 5, 2018, https://www.nytimes.com/2018/07/05/upshot/americans-are-having-fewer-babies-they-told-us-why.html.

2. Schulman, K. "Overdue for Investment: State Childcare Assistance Policies 2018," National Women's Law Center, October 2018.

3. Adamu, M. & Hamm, K. "How Low Childcare Wages Put All Children at Risk," Talk Poverty, Center for American Progress, December 12, 2014, https://talkpoverty.org/2014/12/12/low-child-care-wages/.

4. Katz, L. & Goldin, C. "Mass Secondary Schooling and the State: The Role of State Compulsion in the High School Movement," in "Understanding Long-Run Economic Growth: Geography, Institutions, and the Knowledge Economy," National Bureau of Economic Research: University of Chicago Press, 2011.

5. Batten, D. "The G.I. Bill, Higher Education and American Society." Grove City College Journal of Law and Public Policy 2, no. 1.

6. Barga, M. "The 'Bonus March' (1932): The Unmet Demands and Needs of WWI Heroes." Virginia Commonwealth University Social Welfare History Project. https://socialwelfare.library.vcu.edu/eras/great-depression/bonus-march/

7. Celis, W. "50 Years Later, the Value of the G.I. Bill Is Questioned," The New York Times, June 22, 1994, https://www.nytimes.com/1994/06/22/us/50-years-later-the-value-of-the-gi-bill-is-questioned.html.

8. National Kids Count Data Center. "Children under age 6 with all available parents in the labor force in the United States." Annie E. Casey Foundation, 2017. https://datacenter.kidscount.org/data/tables/5057-children-under-age-6-with-all-available-parents-in-the-labor-force

9. Child Care Aware of America, "The US and the High Cost of Childcare: A Review of Prices and Proposed Solutions for a Broken System," 2018.

10. Purtill, C. & Kopf, D. "The crazy economics of childcare costs in America," Quartz, October 19, 2017, https://qz.com/work/1096890/the-crazy-economics-of-childcare-costs/; see also U.S. Census Bureau, "Childcare Costs on the Upswing, Census Bureau Reports," April 3, 2013, https://www.census.gov/newsroom/press-releases/2013/cb13-62.html

11. Bruenig, M. "Family Fun Pack," The People's Policy Project, Feb. 2019, https://www.peoplespolicyproject.org/projects/family-fun-pack/

12. Schochet, L. & Malik, R. "2 Million Parents Forced to Make Career Sacrifices Due to Problems with Childcare," Center for American Progress, Sept. 13, 2017, https://www.americanprogress.org/issues/early-childhood/news/2017/09/13/438838/2-million-

parents-forced-make-career-sacrifices-due-problems-child-care/.

13. Livingston, G. "Stay-at-home moms and dads account for about one-in-five U.S. parents," Pew Research Center, Sept. 24, 2018, https://www.pewresearch.org/fact-tank/2018/09/24/stay-at-home-moms-and-dads-account-for-about-one-in-five-u-s-parents/

14. Schochet, L. "The Childcare Crisis Is Keeping Women Out of the Workforce," Center for American Progress, March 28, 2019, https://www.americanprogress.org/issues/early-childhood/reports/2019/03/28/467488/child-care-crisis-keeping-women-workforce/

15. Mattingly, M. & Wimer, C. "Childcare Expenses Push Many Families Into Poverty." University of New Hampshire Carsey School of Public Policy (Carsey Research National Fact Sheet #36), Spring 2017.

16. Stevens, K. "Workforce of Today, Workforce of Tomorrow: The Business Case for High-Quality Childcare," U.S. Chamber of Commerce Foundation, June 2017

17. Bishop-Josef, S., et. al. "Want to Grow the Economy? Fix the Childcare Crisis," Council for a Strong America (ReadyNation), January 2019

18. Ibid

19. Rosen, A. & Ellement, J. "Child dies at unlicensed Sturbridge day care center," The Boston Globe, April 12, 2017, https://www.bostonglobe.com/metro/2017/04/12/child-dies-unlicensed-sturbridge-day-care-center/zggn3tIWsZJ0EpdjuFnUGL/story.html.

20. Harvard Center on the Developing Child, "Brain Architecture," https://developingchild.harvard.edu/science/key-concepts/brain-architecture/.

21. Shonkoff, J. P., & Phillips, D. A. (Eds.). (2000). From neurons to neighborhoods: The science of early childhood development. Washington, DC, US: National Academies Press.

22. Stoney, L. "The Iron Triangle: A Simple Formula for Financial Policy in ECE Programs." Alliance for Early Childhood Finance, Oct. 2010.

23. Center for the Study of Childcare Employment, "Early Childhood Workforce Index 2018," University of California, Berkeley, June 2018

24. National Association for the Education of Young Children, "Power to the Profession: Discussion Draft 2, Decision Cycles 345+6," December 2018

25. Miles, K. "Weekend Roundup: Politics Is the Art of the Possible." Huffington Post, July 24, 2017. https://www.huffpost.com/entry/weekend-roundup-76_b_7867298

26. Cohn, J. "The Hell of American Day Care," The New Republic, April 15, 2013, https://newrepublic.com/article/112892/hell-american-day-care.

27. Wang, W. & Wilcox, W.B. The Millennial Success Sequence: Marriage, Kids, and the 'Success Sequence' among Young Adults," American Enterprise Institute (Institute for Family Studies), 2017

28. Moms Rising. "Stories of the Childcare Struggle in America," Feb. 2019. https://s3.amazonaws.com/s3.momsrising.org/images/Childcare_Storybook_Feb_2019.pdf

29. United Way, "United For Alice," https://www.unitedforalice.org/home

30. Harvard Kennedy School Institute of Politics, "Fall 2015 Poll," https://iop.harvard.edu/survey/details/harvard-iop-fall-2015-poll.

31. Wang, W., Parker, K. & Taylor, P. "Breadwinner Moms," Pew Research Center, May 2013, https://www.pewsocialtrends.org/2013/05/29/breadwinner-moms/

32. Michel, S. "Children's Interests/Mothers' Rights: The Shaping of America's Childcare Policy." Yale University, 1999.

33. Michel, S. "The History of Childcare in the U.S.," Social Welfare History Project, 2011, http://socialwelfare.library.vcu.edu/programs/child-care-the-american-history/.
34. Michel, S. "Children's Interests/Mothers' Rights: The Shaping of America's Childcare Policy." Yale University, 1999.
35. Cahan, E. "Past Caring: A History of U.S. Preschool Care and Education for the Poor, 1820–1965." National Center for Children in Poverty (Columbia University), 1989. https://www.researchconnections.org/childcare/resources/2088/pdf.
36. Ibid
37. Cohen, N. "Why America Never Had Universal Childcare," The New Republic, April 24, 2013, https://newrepublic.com/article/113009/child-care-america-was-very-close-universal-day-care
38. Roth, W. "The Politics of Daycare: The Comprehensive Child Development Act of 1971," University of Wisconsin-Madison (Institute For Research on Poverty), Dec. 1976
39. United States Government Printing Office, "Public Papers of the Presidents of the United States, Richard Nixon, 1971"
40. Harbach, M. "Childcare Market Failure," 2015 Utah L. Rev 659 (2015)
41. Neubauer, P. "The Century of the Child," The Atlantic, July 1961, https://www.theatlantic.com/magazine/archive/1961/07/the-century-of-the-child/304098/
42. West, M. "Infant Care." U.S. Department of Labor Children's Bureau, 1914 (Care of Children Series #2). https://www.mchlibrary.org/collections/chbu/3121-1914.PDF
43. Michel, S. "The History of Childcare in the U.S.," Social Welfare History Project, 2011, http://socialwelfare.library.vcu.edu/programs/child-care-the-american-history/.
44. Cahan, E. "Past Caring: A History of U.S. Preschool Care and Education for the Poor, 1820–1965." National Center for Children in Poverty (Columbia University), 1989. https://www.researchconnections.org/childcare/resources/2088/pdf.
45. Piaget, J. "Part I: Cognitive development in children: Piaget development and learning." J. Res. Sci. Teach., 2: 176-186 (1964). doi:10.1002/tea.3660020306
46. Pew Research Center. "The Rise in Dual Income Households," June 18, 2015. https://www.pewresearch.org/ft_dual-income-households-1960-2012-2/
47. Kuhn, M., Schularick, M. & Steins, U. "The Great American Debt Boom, 1949-2013," Discussion paper, University of Bonn, 2017.
48. Desilver, D. "For most U.S. workers, real wages have barely budged in decades." Pew Research Center, Aug. 7, 2018. https://www.pewresearch.org/fact-tank/2018/08/07/for-most-us-workers-real-wages-have-barely-budged-for-decades/.
49. Stone, L. "A radical idea to improve family life in America: babysit your neighbor's kids," Vox, Feb. 5, 2018, https://www.vox.com/the-big-idea/2018/2/5/16972258/us-america-fertility-rates-babysit-child-care-baumol.
50. Thomas, D. & Gorry, D. "Regulation and the Cost of Childcare," Mercatus Center Working Paper (George Mason University), August 2015.
51. "Historical Timeline of Public Education in the US," Applied Research Center, https://www.raceforward.org/research/reports/historical-timeline-public-education-us
52. Encyclopedia of Education. "Common School Movement," The Gale Group (2002), https://www.encyclopedia.com/history/united-states-and-canada/us-history/common-school-movement
53. Goldin, C. "A Brief History of Education in the United States," National Bureau of Economic

Research, Aug. 1999

54. Tyack, D. "The One Best System: A History of American Urban Education." Harvard University Press, 1974.

55. Office of Administration for Children and Families (U.S. Department of Health & Human Services), "CCDF Expenditures Overview for FY2016," https://www.acf.hhs.gov/occ/resource/ccdf-expenditures-overview-for-fy-2016-as-of-9-30-2016

56. Raimondo, G. "State of the State Address Transcript" State of Rhode Island (Office of the Governor), delivered Jan. 15, 2019. http://www.governor.ri.gov/newsroom/speeches/2019/state-of-the-state.php

57. Kaestle, C. "Conflict and Consensus Revisited: Notes toward a Reinterpretation of American Educational History." Harvard Educational Review: September 1976, Vol. 46, No. 3, pp. 390-396.

58. U.S. Census Bureau, "School Spending Per Pupil Increased by 3.2 Percent, U.S. Census Bureau Reports," May 21, 2018, https://www.census.gov/newsroom/press-releases/2018/school-spending.html.

59. Stevens, K. "Workforce of Today, Workforce of Tomorrow: The Business Case for High-Quality Childcare," U.S. Chamber of Commerce Foundation, June 2017

60. Barnum, M. "Here's a list of studies showing that kids in poverty do better in school when their families have more money," Chalkbeat, Sept. 26, 2018, https://chalkbeat.org/posts/us/2018/09/26/list-studies-test-scores-poverty-school-income/.

61. For average impacts of improving teacher quality, see Goldhaber, D. "In Schools, Teacher Quality Matters Most." Education Next, Vol. 16, No. 2 (Spring 2016), https://www.educationnext.org/in-schools-teacher-quality-matters-most-coleman/

62. National Academies of Sciences, Engineering, and Medicine. "A Roadmap to Reducing Child Poverty." Washington, DC: The National Academies Press (2019). doi: https://doi.org/10.17226/25246

63. Centers for Disease Control and Prevention (National Center for Injury Prevention and Control, Division of Violence Prevention). "Essentials for Childhood: Creating Safe, Stable, Nurturing Relationships and Environments for All Children." https://www.cdc.gov/violenceprevention/pdf/essentials-for-childhood-framework508.pdf.

64. Schulte, B. & Durana, A., "The Care Report," New America Foundation, 2016, https://www.newamerica.org/better-life-lab/policy-papers/new-america-care-report/

65. Paschall, K. & Trout, K. "Most child care settings in the United States are homes, not centers." ChildTrends, May 1, 2018. https://www.childtrends.org/most-child-care-providers-in-the-united-states-are-based-in-homes-not-centers

66. Committee for Economic Development of The Conference Board. "Childcare in State Economies - 2019 Update." Produced by RegionTrack, 2019. https://www.ced.org/assets/reports/childcareimpact/181104%20CCSE%20Report%20Jan30.pdf

67. ChildTrends, "Trends in Childcare," 2016, https://www.childtrends.org/indicators/child-care

68. Based on author's analysis of state's publicly reported kindergarten readiness data

69. Christakis, E. "The Importance of Being Little: What Young Children Really Need from Grownups" Penguin Books, 2017

70. Whitehurst, G. "A Good-Enough Early Childhood," The Brookings Institution (Economic Studies at Brookings, Evidence Speaks Reports, Vol 2, #63), Dec. 20, 2018, https://www.brookings.edu/research/a-good-enough-early-childhood/.

71. Oster, E. "Cribsheet: A Data-Driven Guide to Better, More Relaxed Parenting, from Birth to Preschool." Penguin Press: 2019.

72. Institute of Medicine and National Research Council. "Transforming the Workforce for Children Birth Through Age 8: A Unifying Foundation" Washington, DC: The National Academies Press, 2015 https://doi.org/10.17226/19401.

73. Harvard Center on the Developing Child. "InBrief: The Science of Early Childhood Development," https://developingchild.harvard.edu/resources/inbrief-science-of-ecd/.

74. Wong, K. "Why Humans Give Birth to Helpless Babies." Scientific American, Aug. 28, 2012. https://blogs.scientificamerican.com/observations/why-humans-give-birth-to-helpless-babies/

75. Harvard Center on the Developing Child, "What is Early Childhood Development? A Guide to the Science," https://developingchild.harvard.edu/guide/what-is-early-childhood-development-a-guide-to-the-science/

76. Bick, J. & Nelson, C. "Early Adverse Experiences and the Developing Brain." Neuropsychopharmacology. Jan. 2016; 41(1): 177–196.

77. Perry, B.D. "The Boy Who Was Raised As a Dog: And Other Stories from a Child Psychiatrist's Notebook: What Traumatized Children Can Teach Us About Loss, Love and Healing." Basic Books, 2007.

78. Waters, J. "5 questions with the Perigee Fund's Dr. David Willis." Capita Ideas (Medium.com), Aug. 6, 2018. https://medium.com/capita-ideas/5-questions-with-the-perigee-funds-dr-david-willis-b52de235964b

79. Tough, P. "How Children Succeed: Grit, Curiosity, and the Hidden Power of Character." Mariner Books, 2013.

80. Whitehurst, G. "Family Support or School Readiness? Contrasting Models of Spending on Children's Early Care and Learning," The Brookings Institution (Economic Studies at Brookings, Evidence Speaks Reports, Vol 1, #16), April 28, 2016, https://www.brookings.edu/wp-content/uploads/2016/07/Family-support3.pdf.

81. Shonkoff, J. P., & Phillips, D. A. (Eds.). (2000). From neurons to neighborhoods: The science of early childhood development. Washington, DC, US: National Academies Press.

82. Bronfenbrenner, U. "The Ecology of Human Development: Experiments by Nature and Design." Cambridge, Massachusetts: Harvard University Press (1979).

83. Ballabeina, et. al. "Influence of a lifestyle intervention in preschool children on physiological and psychological parameters: Study design of a cluster randomized controlled trial." BMC Public Health 9(1):94, April 2009. Used under Creative Commons License 2.0. https://www.researchgate.net/figure/Ecological-Model-Bronfenbrenners-Ecological-Model-describing-the-environmental_fig2_24247760

84. National Governors Association, "Integrating and Advancing State Prenatal to Age 3 Policies: Report of an Expert Roundtable Conversation," June 2018, https://www.nga.org/wp-content/uploads/2018/11/10-29-18-ED-Report-Prenatal-Age-3-Policies.pdf.

85. Malik, R., Hamm, K., et. al. "America's Childcare Deserts in 2018," Center for American Progress, Dec. 6, 2018, https://www.americanprogress.org/issues/early-childhood/reports/2018/12/06/461643/americas-child-care-deserts-2018/.

86. Harvard T.H. Chan School of Public Health, NPR, & The Robert Wood Johnson Foundation. "Childcare and Health in America." Oct. 2016, https://cdn1.sph.harvard.edu/wp-content/uploads/sites/94/2016/10/Child-Care-and-Health-in-America-Poll-Report_-October-

2016.pdf

87. Tracy, L. "Trying To Find Affordable Childcare Is Not The Job I Wanted." Refinery29, April 2, 2019, https://www.refinery29.com/en-us/2019/04/228243/the-struggle-to-find-good-affordable-child-care

88. Jessen-Howard, S., Malik, R., Workman, S. & Hamm, K. "Understanding Infant and Toddler Childcare Deserts," Center for American Progress, Oct. 31, 2018. https://www.americanprogress.org/issues/early-childhood/reports/2018/10/31/460128/understanding-infant-toddler-child-care-deserts/

89. Kids Count Data Center (The Annie E. Casey Foundation), "Child Population by Age Group in the United States," https://datacenter.kidscount.org/data/tables/101-child-population-by-age-group

90. United States Census Bureau, "Industry Snapshot: Child Day Care Services," 2012. https://thedataweb.rm.census.gov/TheDataWeb_HotReport2/econsnapshot/2012/snapshot.hrml?NAICS=624410

91. Kleiner, S. "Day care for low-income families in South Richmond is set to close in June," Richmond Times-Dispatch, March 2, 2016. https://www.richmond.com/news/local/city-of-richmond/day-care-for-low-income-families-in-south-richmond-is/article_b01aed71-c5f3-5149-9f40-355fb781445e.html

92. Connecticut Voices for Children, "Childcare center closures increased by 55% in 2016-2017 compared to previous year," Sept. 13, 2017, http://www.ctvoices.org/C4Kclosures.

93. Fullbright, L. "6 Investigates: State Of Oklahoma Seeing Decline In Daycares," CBS News on 6 (Tulsa, OK), http://www.newson6.com/story/38631777/6-investigates-state-of-oklahoma-seeing-decline-in-daycares.

94. Grunewald, R. & Davies, P. "Hardly child's play: Times have been even tougher than usual for district child-care providers," FedGazette (Federal Reserve Bank of Minneapolis), July 2011 issue, https://www.minneapolisfed.org/publications/fedgazette/hardly-childs-play

95. Quart, A. "Squeezed: Why Our Families Can't Afford America," Ecco, 2018.

96. Williams, C. "When 'Universal' Childcare Isn't Universally High-Quality," The Atlantic, May 1, 2018, https://www.theatlantic.com/family/archive/2018/05/quebec-child-care-family-leave/559310/

97. Costanzo, R. "Childcare Subsidy: Why Quebec's $7 Per Day Daycare Isn't All It's Cracked Up To Be," The Huffington Post Canada, Sept. 29, 2015, https://www.huffingtonpost.ca/2015/09/29/child-care-subsidy_n_8178184.html

98. Early Childhood Observatory (Observatoire des Tout-Petits). "Early Childhood: The Quality of Educational Childcare Services in Quebec," 2018.

99. Williams, C. "When 'Universal' Childcare Isn't Universally High-Quality," The Atlantic, May 1, 2018, https://www.theatlantic.com/family/archive/2018/05/quebec-child-care-family-leave/559310/

100. Blatchford, A. "Bank of Canada head underlines potential of Quebec childcare for entire country," The Canadian Press, March 13, 2018, https://business.financialpost.com/pmn/business-pmn/bank-of-canada-head-underlines-potential-of-quebec-child-care-for-entire-country

101. Smith, L & Tracey, S. "Childcare is infrastructure. We should treat it that way," Roll Call, March 25, 2019, https://www.rollcall.com/news/opinion/child-care-facilities-infrastructure?mc_cid=c9d5571436&mc_eid=ac6a98f4ef

102. Organization for Economic Cooperation and Development. "Early Childhood Education and Care Policy in Finland." Background report prepared for the OECD Thematic Review of Early

Childhood Education and Care Policy, May 2000, http://www.oecd.org/finland/2476019.pdf

103. Harbach, M. "Childcare Market Failure," 2015 Utah L. Rev 659 (2015)

104. Minnesota Department of Education. "Early Learning Scholarships Program." https://education.mn.gov/MDE/fam/elsprog/elschol/

105. Olorenshaw, V. "Viewpoint: Liberating Motherhood and the Need for a Maternal Feminism," Discovery Society, Issue 30, March 2016, https://discoversociety.org/2016/03/01/viewpoint-liberating-motherhood-and-the-need-for-a-maternal-feminism/.

106. Wang, W. "Mothers and Work: What's 'Ideal'?" Pew Research Center, Aug. 19, 2013. https://www.pewresearch.org/fact-tank/2013/08/19/mothers-and-work-whats-ideal/

107. Ellingæter, A. "Cash For Childcare: Experiences from Finland, Norway, and Sweden," Friedrich Ebert Stiftung, April 2012, https://library.fes.de/pdf-files/id/09079.pdf

108. AARP.org. "Can I Get Paid to Be a Caregiver for a Family Member?" 2017, https://www.aarp.org/caregiving/financial-legal/info-2017/you-can-get-paid-as-a-family-caregiver.html

109. Paquette, D. "The shocking number of new moms who return to work two weeks after childbirth," The Washington Post, Aug. 19, 2015, https://www.washingtonpost.com/news/wonk/wp/2015/08/19/the-shocking-number-of-new-moms-who-return-to-work-two-weeks-after-childbirth/.

110. Neas, K. "Social Security disability fraud is rare," The Hill, Jan. 16, 2014, https://thehill.com/blogs/congress-blog/economy-budget/195559-social-secuity-disability-fraud-is-rare; Rude, E. "The Very Short History of Food Stamp Fraud in America," TIME, March 30, 2017, http://time.com/4711668/history-food-stamp-fraud/

111. Ellingæter, A. "Cash For Childcare: Experiences from Finland, Norway, and Sweden," Friedrich Ebert Stiftung, April 2012, https://library.fes.de/pdf-files/id/09079.pdf

112. Cha, A. "As U.S. fertility rates collapse, finger-pointing and blame follow," The Washington Post, Oct. 19, 2018, https://www.washingtonpost.com/health/2018/10/19/us-fertility-rates-collapse-finger-pointing-blame-follow/.

113. Stone, L. "A radical idea to improve family life in America: babysit your neighbor's kids," Vox, Feb. 5, 2018, https://www.vox.com/the-big-idea/2018/2/5/16972258/us-america-fertility-rates-babysit-child-care-baumol.

114. Mendes, E., Saad, L. & McGeeney, K. "Stay-at-Home Moms Report More Depression, Sadness, Anger." Gallup, May 18, 2012. https://news.gallup.com/poll/154685/stay-home-moms-report-depression-sadness-anger.aspx

115. Afterschool Alliance. "America After 3PM: Afterschool Programs in

116. Demand." Washington, D.C, 2014

117. See, e.g. Leonhardt, M. "The average parent expects to pay almost $1,000 for child care this summer." CNBC.com, June 20, 2019. https://www.cnbc.com/2019/06/19/the-average-parent-expects-to-pay-almost-1000-for-summer-child-care.html

118. See, e.g., McCombs, J.S., et. al. "Making Summer Count: How Summer Programs Can Boost Children's Learning." RAND Education, 2011. https://www.wallacefoundation.org/knowledge-center/Documents/Making-Summer-Count-How-Summer-Programs-Can-Boost-Childrens-Learning.pdf

119. Christakis, E. "The Importance of Being Little: What Young Children Really Need from Grownups" Penguin Books, 2017

120. Butrymowicz, S. & Mader, J. "Childcare Crisis: State's weak oversight puts children in harm's way in Mississippi," The Hechinger Report, Jan. 31, 2016, https://hechingerreport.org/child-care-crisis-states-weak-oversight-puts-children-in-harms-way-in-mississippi/.

121. Hamre, B., Goffin, S., & Kraft-Sayre, M. "Classroom Assessment Scoring System (CLASS) Implementation Guide," Teachstone, Dec. 2009

122. Wisconsin Early Childhood Association & Wisconsin Council on Children & Families. "Youngstar: How Much Does High Quality Cost?" Oct. 27, 2014, http://kidsforward.net/assets/Cost-modeling-one-pager-Oct-27-14.pdf

123. Workman, S. "Where Does Your Childcare Dollar Go?: Understanding the True Cost of Quality Early Childhood Education." Center for American Progress, Feb. 14, 2018, https://www.americanprogress.org/issues/early-childhood/reports/2018/02/14/446330/child-care-dollar-go/.

124. Workman, S. "Where Does Your Childcare Dollar Go?: Understanding the True Cost of Quality Early Childhood Education." Center for American Progress, Feb. 14, 2018,

125. Harris, A.J. "Alabama woman keeps resurrecting shoddy day cares in God's name," Reveal (The Center for Investigative Reporting), April 14, 2016, https://www.al.com/news/2016/04/alabama_woman_keeps_resurrecti.html.l

126. Cohn, J. "The Hell of American Day Care," The New Republic, April 15, 2013, https://newrepublic.com/article/112892/hell-american-day-care.

127. U.S. Administration for Children & Families: Office of Childcare (U.S. Department of Health & Human Services), "Contemporary Issues in Licensing: Enforcement and Approaches with Illegally-Operating Providers," Aug. 2014, https://childcareta.acf.hhs.gov/sites/default/files/public/1408_illegally_operating_providers_final.pdf

128. Zelinski, A. "State rejects calls to reduce childcare ratios." The Houston Chronicle, July 14, 2017. https://www.houstonchronicle.com/news/politics/texas/article/State-rejects-calls-to-reduce-childcare-ratios-8674947.php

129. Barnett, W.S. & Kasmin, R. "Teacher Compensation Parity Policies and State-Funded Pre-K Programs," National Institute for Early Education Research & Center for the Study of Childcare Employment (University of California, Berkeley), 2017.

130. Whitebook, M., Phillips, D., & Howes, C. "Worthy Work, STILL Unlivable Wages: The Early Childhood Workforce 25 Years after the National Childcare Staffing Study," Center for the Study of Childcare Employment (University of California, Berkeley), 2014

131. Barnett, W.S. & Kasmin, R. "Teacher Compensation Parity Policies and State-Funded pre-K Programs," National Institute for Early Education Research & Center for the Study of Childcare Employment (University of California, Berkeley), 2017

132. Schanzenbach, D.W. & Bauer, L. "The long-term impact of the Head Start program," Brookings Institution, Aug. 19, 2016, https://www.brookings.edu/research/the-long-term-impact-of-the-head-start-program/

133. Minnesota Department of Human Services. "Childcare Workforce in Minnesota: 2006 Statewide Study of Demographics, Training and Professional Development," June 2007.

134. Wisconsin Early Childhood Association, "Wisconsin's Childcare Workforce: Wages, Benefits, Education and Turnover of the Professionals Working with Wisconsin's Youngest Children." 2016. https://wisconsinearlychildhood.org/wp-content/uploads/2018/11/2016-Workforce-study.pdf

135. Mitchell, A. "The Cost of Quality Early Learning in Rhode Island: Interim Report," The Rhode Island Early Learning Council, Dec. 2013, https://qrisnetwork.org/state_resource/2014/cost-quality-early-learning-rhode-island-interim-report

136. Vanderloo, L. "Screen-viewing among preschoolers in childcare: a systematic review," BMC Pediatrics, 2014; Loeb, S. "Missing the target: We need to focus on informal care rather than preschool," The Brookings Institution (Economic Studies at Brookings, Evidence Speaks Reports, Vol 1, #19), June 16, 2016, https://www.brookings.edu/wp-content/uploads/2016/07/childcare2.pdf

137. Bowes, M. "Children in unlicensed day cares are 5 times more likely to die," The Richmond Times-Dispatch, Dec. 20, 2014, https://www.richmond.com/news/local/central-virginia/children-in-unlicensed-day-cares-are-times-more-likely-to/article_e9d6588e-ff51-5b2f-a6a1-4a539c69dcce.html

138. For more on gray markets in childcare, see Schulte, B. & Durana, A., "The Care Report," New America Foundation, 2016, https://www.newamerica.org/better-life-lab/policy-papers/new-america-care-report/

139. U.S. Administration for Children & Families: Office of Planning, Research & Evaluation (U.S. Department of Health & Human Services). "National Survey of Early Care and Education Fact Sheet: Who is Providing Home-based Early Care and Education?" 2015, https://www.acf.hhs.gov/sites/default/files/opre/hb_providers_fact_sheet_toopre_041715_508.pdf

140. Virginia Department of Social Services, "General Procedures and Information for Licensure," Effective Oct. 19, 2017

141. U.S. Administration for Children & Families: Office of Childcare (U.S. Department of Health & Human Services), "Contemporary Issues in Licensing: Childcare Licensing Inspection Policies," August 2014, https://childcareta.acf.hhs.gov/sites/default/files/public/1408_inspection_policies_final.pdf

142. Lundeen, "Confessions of a Home Day Care Provider," American Design Club, March 20, 2018, http://www.americandesignclubshop.com/confessions-home-day-care-provider/

143. National Survey of Early Care and Education Project Team. "Characteristics of Home-based Early Care and Education Providers: Initial Findings from the National Survey of Early Care and Education." OPRE Report #2016-13 (2016), Washington, DC: Office of Planning, Research and Evaluation, Administration for Children and Families, U.S. Department of Health and Human Services.

144. Loeb, S. "Missing the target: We need to focus on informal care rather than preschool," The Brookings Institution (Economic Studies at Brookings, Evidence Speaks Reports, Vol 1, #19), June 16, 2016, https://www.brookings.edu/wp-content/uploads/2016/07/childcare2.pdf

145. New York Early Childhood Professional Development Institute & The City University of New York. "Informal Family Childcare Project." http://www.earlychildhoodnyc.org/ifcc/

146. Shivers, E., Yang, C. & Farago, F. "The Arizona Kith and Kin Project Evaluation, Brief #1." Stephen F. Austin State University, Faculty Publications, 2016. https://scholarworks.sfasu.edu/cgi/viewcontent.cgi?article=1010&context=humansci_facultypubs

147. Gibbons, E. "Good Childcare Is Out Of Reach For Too Many. It Doesn't Have To Be This Way." WBUR (Boston, 90.9), Dec. 18, 2018, https://www.wbur.org/cognoscenti/2018/12/18/child-care-costs-elizabeth-gibbons

148. Whelan, C.K. "More American families are doing nanny shares — here's why." Care.com, March 13, 2018. https://www.care.com/c/stories/8596/heres-why-more-american-families-are-

doing-nanny-shares/

149. Walton, A. "How Parents' Stress Can Hurt A Child, From The Inside Out," Forbes, July 25, 2012, https://www.forbes.com/sites/alicegwalton/2012/07/25/how-parents-stress-can-hurt-a-child-from-the-inside-out/#44f69cb66b38

150. Centers for Disease Control and Prevention. "Adverse Childhood Experiences (ACEs)." https://www.cdc.gov/violenceprevention/childabuseandneglect/acestudy/index.html

151. Lu, M. "Get Ready to Get Pregnant: Your Complete Prepregnancy Guide to Making a Smart and Healthy Baby," William Morrow, 2009

152. Harvard Center on the Developing Child. "Toxic Stress." https://developingchild.harvard.edu/science/key-concepts/toxic-stress/

153. Bethune, S. "Money stress weighs on Americans' health," Monitor on Psychology (American Psychological Association), Vol. 46, No. 4, April 2015, https://www.apa.org/monitor/2015/04/money-stress

154. Mullainathan, S. & Shafir, E. "Scarcity: Why Having Too Little Means So Much," Times Books, 2013.

155. Centers for Disease Control and Prevention (National Center for Injury Prevention and Control, Division of Violence Prevention). "Essentials for Childhood: Creating Safe, Stable, Nurturing Relationships and Environments for All Children." https://www.cdc.gov/violenceprevention/pdf/essentials-for-childhood-framework508.pdf.

156. Pew Research Center, "Parenting In America." Dec. 17, 2015, https://www.pewsocialtrends.org/2015/12/17/2-satisfaction-time-and-support/

157. Shapiro, A.F., Gottman, J.M., and Carrere, S. "The baby and the marriage-Identifying factors that buffer against decline in marital satisfaction after the first baby arrives." Journal of Family Psychology, 14(1), 59-70 (2000).

158. Oster, E. "Cribsheet: A Data-Driven Guide to Better, More Relaxed Parenting, from Birth to Preschool." Penguin Press: 2019.

159. Miller, C.C. "The Relentlessness of Modern Parenting." The New York Times, Dec. 25, 2018. https://www.nytimes.com/2018/12/25/upshot/the-relentlessness-of-modern-parenting.html.

160. From Miller, T.R. (2015). Projected outcomes of Nurse-Family Partnership home visitation during 1996-2013, USA. Prevention Science. 16 (6). 765-777, https://www.nursefamilypartnership.org/wp-content/uploads/2017/02/Miller-State-Specific-Fact-Sheet_US_20170405-1.pdf

161. Hunter, L.P. "The Womb Whisperers: Why More More Pregnant Women Are Hiring Doulas." Essence, July 20, 2016, https://www.essence.com/lifestyle/health-wellness/doulas-why-more-pregnant-women-hiring-womb-whisperer/.

162. Santorum, R. & Miller, G. "Opinion: There Are No Losers When We Invest in Early Childcare," Roll Call, June 4, 2018, https://www.rollcall.com/news/opinion/opinion-no-losers-invest-early-child-care.

163. First Five Years Fund, "2016 National Poll," https://www.ffyf.org/2016-poll/

164. Roth, W. "The Politics of Daycare: The Comprehensive Child Development Act of 1971," University of Wisconsin-Madison (Institute For Research on Poverty), Dec. 1976

165. Haidt, J. "The Righteous Mind: Why Good People Are Divided by Politics and Religion," Pantheon, 2013.

166. Pew Research Center, "Parenting In America." Dec. 17, 2015,

https://www.pewsocialtrends.org/2015/12/17/2-satisfaction-time-and-support/

167. Schulte, B. "Making time for kids? Study says quality trumps quantity." The Washington Post, March 28, 2015, https://www.washingtonpost.com/local/making-time-for-kids-study-says-quality-trumps-quantity/2015/03/28/10813192-d378-11e4-8fce-3941fc548f1c_story.html

168. Dew, J., Britt, S. & Huston, S. "Examining the Relationship Between Financial Issues and Divorce," Family Relations, 61: 615-628 (2012). doi:10.1111/j.1741-3729.2012.00715.x

169. Del Mastro, A. "Why Not Pay Women to Stay Home, Raise Children?" The American Conservative, Aug. 24, 2017, https://www.theamericanconservative.com/articles/why-not-pay-women-to-stay-home-raise-children/.

170. Finer, L., et. al. "Reasons U.S. Women Have Abortions: Quantitative and Qualitative Perspectives." Perspectives on Sexual and Reproductive Health, 2005, 37(3):110–118.; Biggs, M.A., Gould, H. & Foster, D.G., "Understanding why women seek abortions in the US." BMC Womens Health. 2013; 13:29. 2013 Jul 5. doi: 10.1186/1472-6874-13-29.

171. Brown, P.T. "Want to reduce abortion rates? Give parents money." The Washington Post, Jan. 26, 2017, https://www.washingtonpost.com/posteverything/wp/2017/01/26/want-to-reduce-abortion-rates-give-parents-money/?utm_term=.f2d4b35131b5.

172. González, L. "The Effects of a Universal Child Benefit." Barcelona Graduate School of Economics (Working Paper #574), Sept. 2011. http://www.oecd.org/els/emp/49115482.pdf

173. Ujifusa, A. "Report: GOP Platform Rejects Publicly Funded pre-K as Government Intrusion." Education Week, July 13, 2016, http://blogs.edweek.org/edweek/campaign-k-12/2016/07/gop_platform_rejects_pre_K_government_intrusion.html

174. Republican National Committee, "Republican Platform 2016."

175. Stevens, K. "Workforce of Today, Workforce of Tomorrow: The Business Case for High-Quality Childcare," U.S. Chamber of Commerce Foundation, June 2017

176. Petters, M. "Text of Mike Petters speech at 2015 Virginia Workforce Conference." The Daily Press, Oct. 6, 2015. https://www.dailypress.com/news/military/hrmilitary-blog/dp-petters-speech-text-story.html

177. Pollitt, K. "Day Care for All." The New York Times, Feb. 9, 2019. https://www.nytimes.com/2019/02/09/opinion/sunday/child-care-daycare-democrats-progressive.html

178. Shambaugh, J., Bauer, L. & Breitwieser, A. "Who is poor in the United States? A Hamilton Project annual report." The Hamilton Project (Brookings Institution), Oct. 12, 2017. https://www.brookings.edu/research/who-is-poor-in-the-united-states-a-hamilton-project-annual-report/

179. Cahalan, M., Perna, L., Yamashita, M., Ruiz, R. &

180. Franklin, K. "Indicators of Higher Education Equity in the United States: 2016

181. Historical Trend Report." Washington, DC: Pell Institute for the Study of Opportunity in

182. Higher Education, Council for Opportunity in Education (COE) and Alliance for Higher

183. Education and Democracy of the University of Pennsylvania (PennAHEAD), 2016.

184. Haertel, E. "Reliability and Validity of Inferences About Teachers Based on Student Test Scores." Educational Testing Service, 2013.

185. Ulrich, R., Schmit, S. & Cosse, R. "Inequitable Access to Childcare Subsidies." CLASP (Center for Law and Social Policy), April 2019. https://www.clasp.org/sites/default/files/publications/2019/04/2019_inequitableaccess.pdf.

186. Jaffe, S. "The Factory in the Family: The radical vision of Wages for Housework." The Nation, March 14, 2018. https://www.thenation.com/article/wages-for-houseworks-radical-vision/

187. Glass, J., Simon, R. W., Andersson, M. A. "The parenthood 'happiness penalty': The effects of social policies in 22 countries." PRC Research Brief 2(7), 2017. doi:https://doi.org/10.15781/T2Z31NT94

188. ZERO TO THREE. "Strolling Thunder™: Rally Recap," May 8, 2018. https://www.zerotothree.org/resources/1839-strolling-thunder-rally-recap

189. U.S. Department of Education, National Center for Education Statistics. "The Condition of Education 2018 (Postsecondary Institution Expenses)," 2018 (NCES 2018-144).

190. Noll, E., Reichlin, L. & Gault, B. "College Students with Children: National and Regional Profiles." Institute for Women's Policy Research, 2017, https://iwpr.org/wp-content/uploads/2017/02/C451-5.pdf.

191. Freedberg, L. "Final count shows Thurmond winner of California schools chief race by 187,000 votes," EdSource, Dec. 9, 2018, https://edsource.org/2018/final-vote-count-shows-thurmond-winner-of-california-schools-chief-race-by-187000-votes/605864

192. Friedman, M. "Capitalism and Freedom: Fortieth Anniversary Edition." University of Chicago Press, 2002.

193. Helburn, S. (Ed.) "The Silent Crisis in U.S. Childcare." The Annals of the American Academy of Political and Social Science Series (Vol 563), May 1999.

194. Malik, R. "The Effects of Universal Preschool in Washington, D.C.," Center for American Progress, Sept. 26, 2018, https://www.americanprogress.org/issues/early-childhood/reports/2018/09/26/458208/effects-universal-preschool-washington-d-c/

195. Watson, B. "A Case Study of the Pre-K For All DC Campaign." Foundation for Child Development (W.K. Kellogg Foundation), 2010. https://www.fcd-us.org/assets/2016/04/Pre-K-for-All-DC-Case-Study.pdf

196. Tobel, C. & Archer, K. "Despite officials' claims, DC hasn't reached universal pre-K," Greater Greater Washington, June 11, 2012, https://ggwash.org/view/12839/despite-officials-claims-dc-hasnt-reached-universal-pre-k.

197. Regenstein, E. "Regenstein: Early Learning Is the Best Way to Close the Achievement Gap. 5 Reasons Districts Prefer to Play Catch-Up Instead," The 74 Million, March 25, 2019, https://www.the74million.org/article/regenstein-early-learning-is-the-best-way-to-close-the-achievement-gap-5-reasons-districts-prefer-to-play-catch-up-instead/.

198. Barnum, M. "How long does a big-city superintendent last? Longer than you might think," Chalkbeat, May 8, 2018, https://www.chalkbeat.org/posts/us/2018/05/08/how-long-does-a-big-city-superintendent-last-longer-than-you-might-think/.

199. All child population figures from the KidsCount Data Center (Annie E. Casey Foundation): https://datacenter.kidscount.org/data/tables/101-child-population-by-age-group

200. U.S. Department of Education, National Center for Education Statistics. "The Condition of Education 2018." (NCES 2018-144)

201. Centers for Medicare & Medicaid Services, "NHE Fact Sheet." https://www.cms.gov/research-statistics-data-and-systems/statistics-trends-and-reports/nationalhealthexpenddata/nhe-fact-sheet.html

202. Currier, E. & Kypa, S. "How the Federal Government Helps Families Meet Childcare Needs," Pew Trusts, Dec. 6, 2017, https://www.pewtrusts.org/en/research-and-

analysis/articles/2017/12/06/how-the-federal-government-helps-families-meet-child-care-needs; The Joint Committee on Taxation (Congress of the United States), "Estimates Of Federal Tax Expenditures For Fiscal Years 2018-2022," Oct. 4, 2018, https://www.jct.gov/publications.html?func=startdown&id=5148

203. Garcia, J., Heckman, J., et. al. "Quantifying the Life-cycle Benefits of a Prototypical Early Childhood Program." IZA Institute of Labor Economics (Discussion Paper), May 2017

204. See, e.g., Martinez, C.A & Perticara, M. "Childcare Effects on Maternal Employment: Evidence from Chile." Poverty Action Lab, 2016. https://www.povertyactionlab.org/sites/default/files/publications/569_Childcare-Effects-on-Maternal-Employment_Chile_CLaudia_August2016.pdf.

205. Malik, R. "The Effects of Universal Preschool in Washington, D.C.," Center for American Progress, Sept. 26, 2018, https://www.americanprogress.org/issues/early-childhood/reports/2018/09/26/458208/effects-universal-preschool-washington-d-c/.

206. U.S. Bureau of Labor Statistics, "Civilian labor force participation rate by age, sex, race, and ethnicity," Oct. 24, 2017, https://www.bls.gov/emp/tables/civilian-labor-force-participation-rate.htm.

207. The World Bank, "GDP (current US$)," https://data.worldbank.org/indicator/NY.GDP.MKTP.CD?locations=US

208. Center for the Study of Childcare Employment, "Early Childhood Workforce Index 2018," University of California, Berkeley, June 2018

209. U.S. Bureau of Labor Statistics, "Retail salespersons and cashiers were occupations with highest employment in May 2015," March 31, 2016, https://www.bls.gov/opub/ted/2016/retail-salespersons-and-cashiers-were-occupations-with-highest-employment-in-may-2015.htm.; U.S. Department of Education, National Center for Education Statistics. "Teacher Attrition and Mobility: Results From the 2012–13 Teacher Follow-up Survey," 2014 (NCES 2014-077), https://nces.ed.gov/fastfacts/display.asp?id=28.

210. Sanders, L. "You're Not the Only One Who's Not Paying Your 'Nanny Tax'." The Wall Street Journal, Oct. 12, 2018. https://www.wsj.com/articles/youre-not-the-only-one-whos-not-paying-your-nanny-tax-1539336600

211. National Partnership for Women & Families. "Labor Force Participation by Gender Overall and in Select Age Groups in all 50 States and the District of Columbia," http://www.nationalpartnership.org/our-work/resources/workplace/paid-leave/caregiving-brief-gender-labor-force-participation-rate-chart.pdf

212. Congressional Budget Office. "Options For Reducing the Deficit: 2019 to 2028 (Impose a Tax on Financial Transactions). https://www.cbo.gov/budget-options/2018/54823

213. Internal Revenue Service, "Tax Gap Estimates for Tax Years 2008–2010," April 2016. https://www.irs.gov/pub/newsroom/tax%20gap%20estimates%20for%202008%20through%202010.pdf

214. Purtill, C. & Kopf, D. "The reason the richest women in the US are the ones having the most kids." Quartz, Nov. 11, 2017, https://qz.com/1125805/the-reason-the-richest-women-in-the-us-are-the-ones-having-the-most-kids/.

215. Hazan, M. & Zoabi, H. "Do Highly Educated Women Choose Smaller Families?" Econ J, 125: 1191-1226 (2015). doi:10.1111/ecoj.12148

216. Haspel, E. "When People Can't Afford Another Child, We Know Big Families Are Only For

The Rich." Romper, Jan. 4, 2019, https://www.romper.com/p/when-people-cant-afford-another-child-we-know-big-families-are-only-for-the-rich-15649230

217. Seligson, H. "The Three-Seat Strollers." The New York Times, April 9, 2014, https://www.nytimes.com/2014/04/10/fashion/The-Growing-Three-Child-Household-in-Manhattan.html.

218. Sapolsky, R. "Behave: The Biology of Humans at Our Best and Worst." Penguin Press, 2017.

219. Costandi, M. "Pregnant 9/11 survivors transmitted trauma to their children." The Guardian, Sept. 11, 2011, https://www.theguardian.com/science/neurophilosophy/2011/sep/09/pregnant-911-survivors-transmitted-trauma.

220. Metz, G., et. al. "Ancestral Exposure to Stress Epigenetically Programs Preterm Birth Risk and Adverse Maternal and Newborn Outcomes." BMC Medicine (2014), 12:121, http://www.biomedcentral.com/1741-7015/12/121.

221. Khazan, O. "Inherited Trauma Shapes Your Health," The Atlantic, Oct. 16, 2018, https://www.theatlantic.com/health/archive/2018/10/trauma-inherited-generations/573055/.

222. Mullainathan, S. & Shafir, E. "Scarcity: Why Having Too Little Means So Much," Times Books, 2013.

223. Levin-Waldman, O. "Income, civic participation and achieving greater democracy." The Journal of Socio-Economics, Vol. 43 (2013), pp. 83-92, https://doi.org/10.1016/j.socec.2013.01.004.

224. Glass, J., Simon, R. W., Andersson, M. A. "The parenthood 'happiness penalty': The effects of social policies in 22 countries." PRC Research Brief 2(7), 2017. doi:https://doi.org/10.15781/T2Z31NT94

225. Hoagwood, K. E., M. J. Rotheram-Borus, M. A. McCabe, N. Counts, H. M. E. Belcher, D. K. Walker, and K. A. Johnson. "The interdependence of families, communities, and children's health: Public investments that strengthen families and communities, and promote children's healthy development and societal prosperity." NAM Perspectives. Discussion Paper, National Academies of Medicine, Washington, DC., 2018, doi: 10.31478/201804a.

226. Philipsborn, R.P. & Chan, K. "Climate Change and Global Child Health." Pediatrics, Vol. 141 (No. 6), June 2018. doi: 10.1542/peds.2017-3774.

227. Marshall, G. "Don't Even Think About It: Why Our Brains Are Wired to Ignore Climate Change," Bloomsbury USA, 2014.

228. Revkin, A. "The Scariest Climate Science of All," Medium, March 16, 2016, https://medium.com/@revkin/around-2006-having-spent-more-than-two-decades-writing-about-the-science-behind-global-warming-i-96a21df2d68e.

229. Last, J. "America's Baby Bust," The Wall Street Journal, Feb. 12, 2013, https://www.wsj.com/articles/SB10001424127887323375204578270053387770718

230. Bruenig, M. "Family Fun Pack," The People's Policy Project, Feb. 2019, https://www.peoplespolicyproject.org/projects/family-fun-pack/

231. Matthew, D. "Child poverty in the US is a disgrace. Experts are embracing this simple plan to cut it." Vox, April 27, 2017, https://www.vox.com/policy-and-politics/2017/4/27/15388696/child-benefit-universal-cash-tax-credit-allowance.

232. The Associated Press, "There's a thriving black market for baby formula," Jan. 7, 2016, https://nypost.com/2016/01/07/theres-a-thriving-black-market-for-baby-formula/

233. Covert, B. "Welcome to America, Where Parents Can't Afford Diapers." The Nation, Aug. 22, 2018, https://www.thenation.com/article/welcome-to-america-where-parents-cant-afford-diapers/

234. Holt, S. "Can Baby Bonds Help Shrink the Wealth Gap?" CityLab (The Atlantic Monthly Group), July 11, 2017, https://www.citylab.com/equity/2017/07/baby-bonds-wealth-gap-boston/533253/

235. Workman, S. "Where Does Your Childcare Dollar Go?: Understanding the True Cost of Quality Early Childhood Education." Center for American Progress, Feb. 14, 2018, https://www.americanprogress.org/issues/early-childhood/reports/2018/02/14/446330/child-care-dollar-go/.

236. See Alliance for Early Childhood Finance, "Cost Modeling." http://www.earlychildhoodfinance.org/finance/cost-modeling.

Note From The Author

Word-of-mouth is crucial for any author to succeed. If you enjoyed the book, please leave a review online—anywhere you are able. Even if it's just a sentence or two. It would make all the difference and would be very much appreciated.

Thanks!
Elliot

About the Author

Elliot Haspel is an early childhood and K-12 education policy expert. He holds an M.Ed. in Education Policy & Management from Harvard's Graduate School of Education. His work has been featured on mediums including *The Washington Post*, *Romper*, *McSweeney's Internet Tendency*, and *The New Republic*. Elliot lives in Richmond, VA with his wife and two spirited young daughters.